Observations
from the Stern

Dale Wheaton

Illustrations by David Whalen

Best wishes Dale Wheaton

Timberdoodle Books

Dedham, Maine

"When Nature Calls" and "How to Tell if the Fish Aren't Biting" have appeared in different form in *The Backlash,* an annual newsletter of Wheaton's Lodge.

The following trademarks appear in this book: A & P, Berlitz, Budweiser, Clorox, Colt, Dardevle, De-Liar, Delta, Fenwick, Flatfish, *Field and Stream,* Kevlar, L. L. Bean, "Mark Trail," Mepps, Monel, Mooselook Wobbler, Nautilus, Orvis, Pikey Minnow, Polaroid, Rapala, Ritz, Scout, Solunar Tables, *Sports Afield,* Tupperware.

10 9 8 7 6 5 4 3 2 1

Library of Congress Catalog Card Number: 94-90879

ISBN 0-9645098-0-6

Published by Timberdoodle Books, P.O. Box 261, East Holden, ME 04429. Additional copies are available for $15.50, postpaid, from the publisher. Discounts available on volume purchases.

Illustrations and Cover Design: David Whalen

Watercolor, Back Cover: Ruth Wheaton

Cartography and Copy Editor: Jane Crosen

Typesetting and Layout: C & C Wordsmiths

Printing: Ellsworth American

*For guides everywhere—
especially the boys Down East who spend
their days in a Grand Laker.*

Acknowledgments

I wish to thank Dan and Kay Serebrakian, Mark Danforth, Bob Kay, John Trainor, and Fred Turner for their comments on earlier drafts. David Whalen, whose hand struggles to keep up with his head, helped make this project a lot of fun. Jane Crosen, Jim and Char Chandler, and Tom Gsell were instrumental to the production of the book, and most kind to a neophyte. I also want to thank my mother, Ruth Wheaton, for putting up with a lifetime of guide stories. There is no mention of women guides in this book, because there are few in my area, and this is not a slight to the many competent guides who are women. If remarks in this book are offensive to anyone, they are unintentional.

Contents

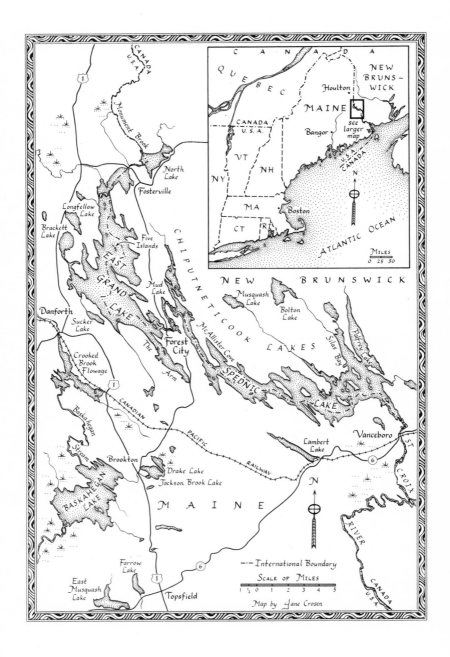

Map by Jane Crosen

Introduction

his little book is about guides and guiding, and though
its setting is in eastern Maine, it has to do with guides
everywhere. It is a guide's perspective on fishing for
smallmouth bass and landlocked salmon with people "from
away," and includes tales about hunting and other things that
happen in the wild. I am a guide, which should absolve me
from any literary criticism.

Guides have long held a special place in the sporting lore
of this country. Their adeptness at finding and outfoxing quarry
has long been acknowledged, as is the unique array of physical
skills they employ. These skills are as diverse as poling a canoe
up a set of rips, making a perch chowder in the wild, or extract-
ing a hook from a client's finger. But that is only part of it.

Maine guides are an independent and free-spirited lot,
their individualism sometimes running to the peculiar. The
choice of a lifestyle far removed from the fame and fortune of a
busy world evokes the quiet admiration of many folks caught
up in economic protocol, for they sense these men understand
something basic about life and have bought into it. Guides
view wild critters as friendly adversaries in some grand game,
taking great relish in tricking them into fatal errors while
drawing their clients into the passion of the chase. Guides also
like to chew on the butts of day-old cigars.

The essence of guiding is, above all, making it fun and enjoyable for the client. This is easier if the fish and game cooperate, although the guide can't rely on that. He must be able to read his clients' interests and temperaments, and fashion the outdoor experience accordingly. This means being adventurous some days, more restrained other days. He must be courteous, know when to offer assistance, and know when to keep his mouth shut. He must know how to entertain, when to kibitz, and when to back off. In short, he must establish good rapport with his clients and allow his personality to reveal itself. You can't be a good guide if you are not a good companion.

Sportsmen and sportswomen come to Maine each year to take a breather from the pace of urban living and to enjoy the tranquility of unspoiled lakes and streams. They are drawn by Maine's abundance of native fish, which sometimes bite and sometimes don't. Whether they do is not terribly important. The lakes are a glacial mix of deep and shallow bodies of water ringed by forests that still exist in the minds of tourists who are unfamiliar with the efficiency of modern tree-harvesting techniques. You can still get away from people here, and that is the main idea. You can also still get lost.

Many of these good folks stay at a traditional sporting camp, a rustic institution of the Maine woods that dates back to the mid-1800s. Here you can get a comfortable cabin and home-cooked meals, and get to know the local mosquitoes on a first-name basis. Staying at a lodge is like taking a step back in time, which is precisely why people come. It has nothing to do with the fact that the owners are slow to make improvements.

Most lodges have a contingent of local guides who take their clients, known in Maine as "sports," out into the wild for brook trout, bass, or other game fish. After the fishing season, guides turn their attention to partridges, ducks, deer, bear, or whatever. Guides enjoy their work, especially if the only alternative involves a chainsaw. It also keeps them out of the homeless shelters. In Maine, most guides continue to ply their trade until the day they die unless they become too frail to break the egg in the coffee. Few other people enjoy the same affection for their occupations.

The guide/sport relationship often develops into a friend-ship that lasts a lifetime. Each day afield is an adventure, and sharing these adventures as companions and equals bonds people of vastly different backgrounds. My summers are a ka-leidoscope of friends who share my canoe from one year to the next. They, like me, consider these moments spent outdoors the highest and best use of time.

It has been said that guests come to lodges for a change and a rest: The guide gets the change and the lodge gets the rest. This, of course, is not true, since nearly everyone carries plastic nowadays. Even in the old days, when everything was paid in cash, we made sure that folks had plenty of toll money. I can't understand why people make those vicious remarks.

The guides in Washington County all use Grand Lake canoes, a twenty-foot square-stern model ideal for fishing salmon and smallmouths in big lake country. The craft origi-nated in the little sporting village of Grand Lake Stream in the early 1920s. It has changed very little over the years, except to accommodate slightly larger motors and all the paraphernalia people feel they have to take with them nowadays. These canoes are comfortable to fish out of, and the shape of their hull allows them to be paddled in shallow water during the bass spawning season.

I come from a family of guides and sporting camp people in eastern Maine with roots in Grand Lake Stream. My wife and I operate a fishing lodge that was started by my folks in 1952, and my brother has camps nearby. Wheaton's Lodge is located on East Grand Lake in Forest City, a village that straddles the international border between Maine and New Brunswick, Canada. Lakes and streams are all around us. There are fewer than thirty year-round residents here, includ-ing the dogs. Summers are busier with the return of retired residents who went south for the winter, summer people, fish-ing folks, and guides who found work elsewhere to tide them over. Still, the "City" in Forest City is pretty deceiving.

My two brothers and I learned to guide at an early age, not because we knew anything about it but because our father needed an extra warm body in the stern of a guide canoe.

There were days when we resisted, either because we had heard of a good trout brook or because some pretty young thing was summering in town, but Dad's size-nine boot quickly brought us back into focus. Eventually, we came to learn a little bit about guiding.

Most of the characters who appear in this book are men who guide with me out of Forest City, or whom I have had the privilege of guiding with in earlier years. We have shared many triumphs and much humility together. These fellows are good friends, or at least they were before I went and published this thing.

Observations
from the Stern

A Little Luck
Comes in Handy

A ny guide will tell you how certain clients are born with an uncanny advantage in terms of good luck, while others simply missed the boat. With some parties you know that things will turn out okay, because they always do and for no other reason. This is not to say a guide should blunder off into the field relying only on his clients' good fortune to guarantee a successful outing; that would be a mite risky. On the other hand, sometimes luck is all you have to work with.

The Schweitzers were an elderly couple from New York who came to the lodge twice each season. They were intelligent, well-educated people, she being an active novelist and he a retired attorney, and they had traveled all over the world. They were good-natured people and fun to be with, especially if you could get on their intellectual plane, which, for me, was not often. They were also, without question, the world's very worst fishermen.

An open-face spinning reel in Gertrude's hands was a disaster waiting to happen. Despite a lifetime of fishing vacations, she could never quite remember whether the line went out when the bail was open or when it was closed. Not only did she not know where her casts were going, she was not even clear on where she wanted them to go. Intermittently, her casts would end in a splat three feet from the rod tip, land behind the canoe because the line slipped off her finger too soon, or spear straight up in the air. She inflicted terror on the occasional unsuspecting seagull, and sent several of my good bass plugs so far into the woods I never found them. Her better casts landed in the lake somewhere.

Stan was no better. Each cast was the product of tremendous effort and concentration, but generally wound up some distance from where it was intended. He had a mannerism of wrinkling up his nose and squinting his eyes whenever he confronted a concept he did not understand. He would become pensive and focused, whether he was considering Aristotle or the anti-reverse, but while he probably figured out the old Greek he faltered on the subtleties of his reel. Many times I watched him study his target, consider his reel, double-check his grip and finger position, then drill his cast God knows where. The lure would sometimes loft high into the wind—which, incidentally, he never allowed for—and end up landing somewhere back in the canoe, followed by forty feet of monofilament. At this point he would examine the water for the whereabouts of his lure, until distracted by all the line draped around his body.

Stan and Gertrude probably never realized there were bass lures other than floating plugs, since we didn't dare tie anything else on their lines. Jigs and spinners were out of the question, even when the bass demanded them. Gertrude had no idea how deep the water was where she was casting, and I don't believe she suspected it was a factor. Stan had a tendency to yank whenever he felt resistance, and that was usually real estate.

Needless to say, whenever the fishing hinged on some semblance of precision casting, things got tough for the guide. I remember my father pulling his hair out in frustration during the bass spawn, ultimately resorting to trolling in the hopes of catching the "village idiot," as Dad called him. Normally he was able to catch enough to stink up the frypan, and the Schweitzers were happy.

When Jana and I purchased the lodge, the Schweitzers somehow became my clients to guide. Dad said it was their custom to fish with the lodge owner, and I didn't question it, but in retrospect the Old Man pulled a fast one. He guided another twelve years and not once discussed the switch within hearing range.

One August they came to fish smallmouths with live bait, as they especially enjoyed frog fishing. Our first day out was a beauty. A cold front had settled into eastern Maine and the wind was blowing from the northwest at twenty knots.

I resigned myself to fishing places offering enough lee to hold anchor, never mind whether we ever caught fish there. True to form, the bass were not feeding and it didn't take long to fish through each available shelter. After ten or more sterile spots I anchored beside a rocky shoal, and by some stroke of luck, hit the jackpot. For nearly two hours we caught smallmouths in the three-pound class until it was time to cook lunch. I did not make much ado over our success, but secretly thanked someone upstairs for His kindness.

Fortunately, a lunch ground was located on the sheltered side of an island a half mile away. We went there and unloaded our gear, and I started to prepare lunch. The wind roared through the treetops, tearing green leaves from the branches, and I could see from our protected spot that the whitecaps were blowing into spray. Without hurrying things any, I tried to chart an itinerary for the afternoon fishing. As a matter of ethics, most guides in our area will rest a bunch of fish for a few days after working them over in good shape. But the options were few. I doubt if any other morons in Washington County were out fishing that day, let alone catching anything, so why argue with good fortune? Sliding the canoe into the lake after lunch, I headed right back to the spot we had just fished.

When the anchor fetched up, Gertrude started scanning the shoreline and nearby landmarks. She looked fore and aft and all about her.

"We've never fished here, Stanley, have we?" she stated. "Woodie never brought us to this spot."

Stanley also looked all around him, his nose wrinkling and his eyes squinting. After careful examination of his surrounds, he responded.

"You are right, dear. This is the first time we have ever fished here."

The fish had not moved, and I didn't say a word.

On another occasion, we were motoring our way toward the landing on Spednic Lake late one June afternoon, having spent the greater part of the day caught on bottom. The wind had swung to the southwest and a misty rain was sneaking over my shoulder. As we started to cross a deep basin I suggested we let out some streamer flies on the chance that a salmon might take. Fine.

I rigged Gertrude with a Gray Ghost, balanced it, let out thirty or so feet of line, set her drag, and passed her the rod. After setting Stan up with another pattern, I tied a streamer on my fly rod and dropped it a few feet back in the wake to see how it was riding.

Suddenly a salmon exploded four feet into the air at the end of the prop wash. It was a damn nice fish and just about scared the life out of me. I turned quickly and shouted, "Who's got him? Who's got him?"

Gertrude looked at me with a blank expression. Stan's nose was wrinkled, his upper lip drawn up underneath it. His rod was doubled over, the tip surging.

"I've got bottom," he said.

"No, Stan, you've got a nice salmon. We're in sixty feet of water. You can't catch bottom this way." He continued to look puzzled. The salmon made another spectacular leap behind me, and this time both of them saw it.

I immediately retrieved my line and had Gertrude do likewise, setting both rods on the thwarts and out of the way. The salmon sounded and took drag. I shut the motor off and pulled up the lower unit to avoid the risk of clipping Stan's line in the prop. The canoe shifted sideways to the wind and we went into a quiet drift.

Again the salmon burst from the water like a missile, this time to starboard and upwind. Normal. Stan's nose started to wrinkle.

"Whose fish is that?" he asked. "Gertrude, is that your fish?"

"Gertrude is not fishing, Stan! Our lines are in." Under other circumstances I probably would have elected not to answer that question, but I wanted to catch the salmon.

Then Gertrude piped in. "You are right, Stanley, that cannot be *your* fish. Your fish is back there." She pointed over the stern to where the salmon had first jumped before we began our drift.

With that exchange, I thought it best not to join the dialogue and instead concentrate on the salmon. Stan's glasses by this time had become so fogged up in the drizzle that he was unable to see. But he sensed from my excitement he was dealing with a truly worthwhile fish. He played that fish with his jaw set and his arms frozen in position, having no idea where the salmon was or what it was up to. If the fish sounded, his rod bowed downward; when the salmon streaked off the bow, his rod curled upward. At least three times the line went dead slack. The salmon jumped once on the opposite side of the canoe, causing Gertrude to swivel around and setting off another round of questions. Stan gripped his rod resolutely, reeling and backing off as I instructed. He was great.

We finally landed that fish, after nearly half an hour and plenty of anxious moments. It was a female fish weighing just shy of five pounds, a pretty landlock. I'm not sure who was more exhausted, the salmon or us.

I cranked up the motor and headed home, my chest all puffed out. A serene smile covered Stan's face. Who said anything about luck?

Getting Ready

F ishing guides arrive mossy-eyed early each morning at sporting camps throughout eastern and northern Maine, in dire need of one more cup of coffee to erase the memory of yesterday's fishing and to summon enough strength to face the day's weather report. They arrive about the time their sports are having breakfast, giving them some leeway to take stock and shake off a heavy head.

Virtually all a guide's worldly possessions are in his canoe or pickup truck, leaving only the "perishables" to be gathered daily. These include gas, lunch, bait, perhaps some dry firewood if it's monsoon weather, or ice if it's the Fourth of July. Most guides reflect for a moment on what they forgot yesterday morning, and this usually helps them get their stuff together.

About the only real challenge involves the matter of bait, especially if it is mid-summer and the bass have turned up their noses to artificials. Each guide knows his success is related to the quality of bait he can muster up, and the available *good* bait on any given day around the lodge is finite. The other guides may be his closest friends, but not when it comes to divvying up the bait. Friendship has its limits.

The plan is to get to the bait cages before the other guides. This can involve a complex strategy of deceptive and evasive maneuvers intended to delay the others while getting to the bait undetected. It is appropriate and acceptable, for example, to suggest to another guide that his outboard is leaking gear grease or that his truck is on fire. Under no circumstances can you be seen strolling to the dock area, bucket in hand, for this will immediately alert your peers and cause all the good bait to be shared. A smarter approach might be to wrap your bucket in a heavy raincoat; walk into the lodge lobby, through the kitchen, and out a rear door; sneak through the generator shed and over a woodpile; thence crawl underneath the camp porches until you get within range of the bait. At the right moment, sprint to the cages, grab a net, and start scooping. If you are a guide, no one will think this behavior strange.

Down East smallmouths eat nightcrawlers, minnows, frogs, crayfish, leeches, hellgrammites, other insects, and anything else small enough to swallow. Bait dealers and lodges, however, stock only those critters which guides are not afraid to touch. You cannot buy leeches, hellgrammites, or salamanders in eastern Maine.

If you are the first guide to the minnow cage and it is freshly stocked, it is a sure bet that one of the sports' kids has run off with the bait net and left it wherever he happened to be when the dinner bell rang. By the time you recover it, all advantage has been lost and four other guides are peering into the cage like blue herons in a salt marsh. If you are the first one to the frog box, the bait man didn't come that day. If you are the last, all that are left are dinosaurs.

Whenever a new shipment of minnows arrives at a lodge the first ones to get wind of it are the local minks and raccoons. A raccoon can single-handedly lap up enough shiners at one sitting to disrupt the camp, ruin several days' fishing, evoke the wrath of the guides, negate the lodge's profit, and cause a run on nightcrawlers. Guests wonder why the camp owner likes to shoot the cute little creatures.

After the bait is taken care of, guides get together to exchange lies and implausible stories. Each morning, guides relate amusing tales and anecdotes from yesterday's outing, pass along any bits of knowledge they deem irrelevant, dis-

cuss their sport's precision casting, and pick on each other. This is the lodge's brain trust.

A guide fortunate enough to boat a trophy fish never speaks at the next convocation, assuming a quiet dignity and standing well to the outside perimeter of conversation. Silence is a guide's way of gloating. He knows that word of his catch traveled faster than dirt at a Tupperware party and by demeanor wishes to suggest it was no big deal. The other guides know better, but honor him by not asking questions to which they will receive false and misleading answers, in the hope that one day they, too, may glow in the same feigned respect.

The morning session ends abruptly when sports begin to trickle out of breakfast. A guide likes to meet his people as soon as they leave the dining room to banter and discuss plans for the day. He imparts every impression of being ready to go, whether he is or not, since he knows very well that his sports must make their morning constitutional, collect their belongings, and convey them to the truck or canoe. It is important to communicate the sense that any delay is due to the sports, establishing a psychological advantage from the outset. Now the guide must scurry around in earnest to prepare for the day.

The camp owner introduces new parties to their guide, having made his assignments beforehand. How he pairs up sports to guides is beyond the understanding of sane and rational people but nonetheless seems to make sense to him.

Nothing is ever simple. If the wind is howling from the northwest, the chances are your sport will turn out to be a popping-bug fisherman. During such cold fronts there exist only a few square feet of lee in Washington County, with the wind flowing in the same direction as the glacier that carved out these water bodies. Any fishable waters probably don't hold fish, you can't turn a fly over in the wind, the bass have lockjaw, and certainly nothing will feed on the surface under such conditions. With a spin fisherman you might have a long shot at catching a stupid fish now and then, but that is not to be.

Murphy's Law doesn't stop there. You can bet that if the salmon are biting, your people will insist on fishing for bass. If the bass are biting, your people will want to fish for salmon. If everything is biting, your people have to return early, either to make a phone call or meet the Delta flight in Bangor. If nothing is biting, your man is probably a writer from *Field and Stream.*

Regardless, it is up to the guide to be friendly and optimistic. However the day might end up, it should start solidly. There are lots of mornings when you would just as soon bury yesterday's scorecard, and nothing affords you that privilege like a new party. Instead of lying, you can just beat around the bush a little until the folks get to know you better. Besides, the fish have to eat sometime.

Guides and their sports naturally like to size one another up. Since this is the guide's turf, the client is at a great disadvantage, but we don't have any trouble with that.

Each guide likes to have a look at his client's equipment. A decent reel with a smooth drag, properly spooled and matched to the rod, will raise your spirits. But when the guy spends ten minutes chipping the rust off his father's metal tackle box, there is usually no sense in taking it along. If his fly reel is mounted upside down, or if the knot connecting the fly line to the leader is the size of a watermelon, it may be a good idea to make a closer inspection. The situation is dangerous if the fellow's spin-cast reel is on his fly rod, his inventory of lures consists of four large Dardevles and six bobbers, or when his camera is bigger than his tackle box. If his line is threaded through the keeper, good luck.

A guide never assumes his clients are well-to-do, even if their equipment is expensive. People who can afford it hire much more attractive company than guides.

Once the client's fishing gear is squared away, the deficiencies having been replaced with working alternatives and the absurd having been graciously condemned to the cabin, a spot check is made of the little items—sunglasses, sunscreen, fly repellent, prescription medication, etc. The guide ultimately inquires about raingear.

Greenhorns think it never rains on vacation. Most of the others forget to consider the effects of wind and spray when quartering the waves on an open lake. Folks who do not understand Maine weather assume that if the sun is shining when they leave the dock there will be no need for raingear, when it could be raining like hell an hour later. The more enlightened bring a raincoat but are unaware that it also rains on the lower half of their body, a fact that is apparent to them after sitting waterlogged in an open boat for eight hours. They also find that sneakers are worse than bare feet on a rainy day.

How late parties stay out on rainy days is proportional to the quality of their raingear. Guides like to see raingear good enough to allow an earnest effort without their sports being miserable, but not so good that they will want to spend the night in the canoe. People who enjoy doing things outdoors soon learn that a rainsuit they can read the newspaper through is not worth the $3.79 they spent for it. Most guides carry duct tape for these poor souls, and also carry their old leaky suits stashed in the bow. A guide whose raincoat is worse than his sport's will die at an early age from hypothermia.

When the guides and their parties are finally ready to push off, everyone wishes each other good luck. No one offers to be more explicit than that.

How to Tell
if the Fish Aren't Biting

A mong a guide's myriad skills is his uncanny ability to recognize when the fish are not biting. This talent escapes many of today's rank-and-file fishermen, who are conditioned to believe that a poor day of fishing beats their best day at work. They may fail to notice whether the rod is bending. Guides are more perceptive. For them, a good day at work beats the hell out of a lousy day of fishing.

A good guide can tell if fish are not biting long before dusk. He sees it in the faces of his sports; he feels the void in his stomach or the bruise to his dignity. These are not new sensations, but ones he would just as soon do without.

Certain omens suggest when the fishing is poor. These signs are so subtle that probably only an experienced angler can pick them up quickly, but I will mention a few so others might get the hang of it.

First and always, the nature of the fishing is evident by the nature of the conversation in the boat. This is usually a dead giveaway. As the fishing deteriorates, the dialogue between sports and guide tends to lose its electricity, starts to ramble, and ultimately becomes strained.

In the early stages of slow fishing, the conversation turns to loons and eagle nests, to Gray Ghosts and Nine-Threes, and eventually to the mating dance of the Eastern water beetle. Guides refer to this as the "Honeymoon Phase"—there is still hope. But when the sport begins to suggest alternative baits and other spots to try, the problem has become serious. The guide now knows he is on borrowed time. Having fished every square inch of these waters day in and day out for thirty years, under every sort of condition, using every invention known to mankind, the guide knows he has little time to produce a fish using plausible techniques before he must defer to the impossible to appease his sport.

A few hours without a strike can bring dialogue to a screeching halt. Guides call this the "Desperate Stage." Lack of conversation correlates to lack of fish. The only stage beyond this is when the guide begins muttering to himself in some unintelligible primal tongue.

Guides are particularly grateful when sports break the silence to tell them how pathetic the fishing really is, for it confirms what the guide suspected. Constant queries such as "When will they start biting?" or "Is it always this slow?" help to reinforce the guide's pride in knowing the answers to esoteric questions. Inquiries like "When are you going to take us to your good spots?" garner the affection of every guide, since they demonstrate confidence in his depth of knowledge. "How long have you been doing this?" affords the guide a chance to discuss his career. Such lines of questioning help keep a guide focused, making for a really enjoyable day.

Lunchtime is a good time for the sports to refine their skills, particularly if the guide happens to join up with another guide and his party. One can soon determine if the malaise is general or specific. Misery in this respect loves company, but only conditionally.

Close observation is warranted if the guide prepares a shore lunch. The novice fisherman can learn much about how good the fishing is by taking inventory of the frypan. See whether the guide feels any need to wash scales from his hands or jackknife. Note how quickly lunch is prepared. A

13

shore lunch that may normally take an hour to prepare and consume can subtly be dragged out to two hours without the slightest hint of stalling or inefficiency. The guide reckons a short afternoon of terrible fishing is superior to a long one.

In his book *To Hell with Fishing* (Appleton-Century, 1945), Ed Zern said, "In the evening, guides sit around the campfire and spit in it. They like to hear the sizzle. After a day of fishing, it makes sense."

Guides often gauge the day's success by the hardness of the stern seat. No guide notices the oak slats under his behind given a regular flow of boated fish, missed strikes, and a few fish of bragging size. But when the slats start cutting furrows perpendicular to the one that is anatomically correct, things have definitely slowed down. Two hours without a hit can actually damage the nerve endings in one or both cheeks, cause the shoulders to sag, and give the face a drawn and haggard appearance. When guides ask their sports to hand them a boat cushion, they are also mentally updating their résumés.

Trolling for trout or landlocked salmon normally involves some downtime, but hopefully these intervals are brief and terminate before the next ice age. By closely observing the sports and their apparatus from the stern seat, I have come to recognize clear signs that the landlocks are not biting. Women begin to read novels. Spiderwebs appear along the rod guides. The bow angler's reverie turns into a snore. My forearm starts to atrophy.

Slow fishing is more difficult to detect when casting for smallmouths, since the canoe is in motion and everyone is active. Nevertheless, I look for clues. Moss shows up on the guy's camera case. Your fly fisherman is practising his nail knot or, worse, he is picking his nose while staring directly at you. The Budweiser lure comes out. And if all the lures in your tackle box are wet but the net is dry, you can bet the bass are not at frenzy stage.

I once watched a fly-fisherman carefully working a section of remote stream, but never bothered to approach him and ask about the fishing. His fingers had acupuncture welts from changing flies, and the mosquitoes were taking no interest in his creel. When he began rolling rocks over along the bank while furtively looking upstream and down, I felt it best to retreat to my trail.

And there are other indications. If you bought two dozen shiners this morning at the bait shop and twenty-three are still doing laps in the bucket, things are quiet. The whitecaps in your bait bucket may explain why. You may also have noticed that the best fight you had from a fish all day was from the minnow.

If you are still unsure, smell your hands. Here, bad news is good news and vice versa. If you can still detect a trace of your after-shave lotion, figure on hamburgers for supper. When my wife once complained about my vile fishy odor, I told her not to worry about the mortgage payment so long as I smelled that way.

Even on slow days in the canoe, talk resumes late in the afternoon and takes on a philosophical tone. The woman finishes her novel and rejoins the conversation. The guide smiles and notes how good the fishing was, even if the catching was lousy. A sense of levity returns. Everyone reels up, and the canoe is turned for the landing.

Sporting camp owners find it difficult to acknowledge days like these, except in the privacy of their bedrooms. Guides deal with their despair the only way they know how, through denial and conditioned memory loss. Another night with the depressed-guide support group. . . .

Catching Bottom

A good hook set contributes to a higher percentage of strikes resulting in hooked fish. Unless the hook punctures the bony structure inside the fish's mouth, the hold is tenuous. It is common to see anglers, especially those who only fish now and again, give a strong pull instead of a sharp tug. This only infuriates the fish and causes him to immediately dump the lure. A little slack line, and away he goes.

For this reason, guides always appreciate a sport with a firm set. I did catch hell one time when I complimented a lady on hers, but she eventually got over it.

Sometimes people get a little carried away. They may yank so hard that they snap the leader, losing not only a nice salmon but your favorite streamer. One of Pete Pipine's clients, trolling a Mooselook Wobbler on East Grand, jerked hard enough to tear the upper jaw section completely off a salmon —and then trolled it another six miles thinking he had missed the fish clean. Occasionally they yank so hard that the rod shatters, in which case they blame Fenwick or Orvis.

But my favorite is when people yank on real estate. For a few brief moments you see the climax of anticipation and enthusiasm, the glory of the set, the knowing that the fish has been solidly hooked, the feel of heavy resistance. The lights come on, the music plays. Hopefully, the hook will disengage or the line will snap, preserving a precious moment in the whole trip, and the guide can shrug in sympathy.

Ordinarily, the hook holds. Instead of identifying the resistance on the line, be it animal, vegetable, or mineral, it is more fun to rear back and yank with all your might. How folks think a guide can disengage a hook set half an inch into solid granite is beyond me.

Guides in eastern Maine normally paddle their Grand Lakers along the rocky shorelines while their sports cast for spawning smallmouths. Bassboat owners do not understand why guides continue to use these traditional craft, but part of it is explained by the relative ease with which a guide can retrieve a lure that is snagged on bottom. Without the ability to do this, many guides would run out of tackle in the first couple hours of fishing.

BEAUTIFUL, STANLEY, NOW YOU'VE DONE IT!
YOU'RE DRAINING THIS NICE MAN'S LAKE.

Some days a guide can only cover fifty yards of lake-shore in a forenoon, because more time and distance is consumed to recover lures than to address new waters. It can require the patience of Job. Even the bass get a little uppity after awhile. And the bottom looks like the aftermath of an Army Corps of Engineers project.

Whenever the guide starts the motor or pulls anchor to move to another area, someone will invariably take "one last cast" and get hung up. When you paddle over to get the first guy freed, his buddy will cast into the shallows and get hung up, too. One of the younger guides paddled back and forth in a quarter acre of Baskahegan Lake for most of a week, waiting for that moment when both sports were simultaneously free of bottom. Had there been a pizza joint within a hundred miles, he would have ordered out.

One apparent explanation for this behavior lies in the uniqueness of Maine lakes which, unlike water bodies in other states, get shallower as you get closer to shore. The water a few inches off shore, you see, tends to be only a few inches deep. Sports are not used to this morphometry. Evidently, in other parts of the country the water drops immediately to eight feet and features a smooth bottom incapable of snagging lures, allowing a person to shower the vicinity with casts without fear of obstruction. Maine lakes also are not chlorinated.

Just after ice-out in 1987 we all watched one of the greatest rod and reel encounters in recent history. Mark Danforth and his party were trolling for landlocks on East Grand when one of his sports hooked a mighty fish near Togue Rock. The fellow's rod bowed in a deep arc as the canoe drifted gently southward, parallel to the Canadian shore. It was a classic battle of wills and determination as the fellow would gain line for awhile, then the drag would sing as the adversaries distanced themselves. An hour elapsed, and other guides and fisherman edged closer to witness the event. Observers agreed it was a trophy togue, for each time it ran it headed directly for bottom and made no attempt to jump.

More boats stopped to see the great fight, and Bud Brooks, one of the other guides, took a larger dip net over to

Mark. Another man captured the whole thing on video. My sport, Jack Hill, grumbled because he had been with Mark the previous three days and was now missing the fight of a lifetime.

Finally, as the angler's wrists were about to concede, the quarry surrendered to the rod. It turned out to be a rock, some ten inches in diameter and about twelve pounds in weight, tenaciously hooked on Mark's spoon. Once netted, the rock made not so much as a quiver and lay in the bottom of the boat totally exhausted. The other boats vanished.

That evening an awards ceremony in the lodge dining room acknowledged both guide and sport. Certificates of merit were presented for three distinct fishing achievements: Largest Rock Caught Trolling (Maine State Record), Longest Time Recorded in Playing a Game Rock (63 minutes, 30 seconds), and Heaviest Catch of the Year (Lodge citation). Togue Rock is now referred to as Rock Rock.

If the party is stream fishing from a canoe, the sport never gets his fly or lure fetched on bottom unless it is upstream of the canoe. When lake fishing, it is upwind. This is done mainly out of consideration for the guide's health and fitness.

A guide appreciates the opportunity to build upper body strength, and this occurs whenever he has to urgently reverse direction and paddle or pole the canoe against heavy current. Since most guide canoes lack Nautilus equipment, and many don't even have the basic stuff such as a pull-up bar, retrieving upstream lures provides a welcome workout. It gives tone to the pectorals, triceps, and rectus abdominus. The cardiovascular benefits are terrific.

Given the desirability of exercise, I will suggest a few tips to maximize the guide's workout. For example, if you cast directly upstream you should rapidly strip as much line as possible from the reel, to allow the fly or lure to sink with the current. If an open-face reel is used, simply open the bail and count to a billion. If casting downstream, allow as much slack as possible; do not reel. By allowing the canoe to drift over the line you can add variation to the exercise regimen. Also, *never* tell the guide that the lure is caught until practically all the line has paid off the spool, as this not only increases the intensity of the workout but builds character as well.

When bait fishing, women often ask how they will know when they reach bottom. With a quarter ounce of lead, they can't miss it. My father guided a fellow who was able to snag bottom in forty feet of water with only thirty feet of line. Most anglers never achieve this level of proficiency.

Sometimes you are forced to rig your sports with floating lures, even though spinners and jigs are working much better. This is done in the interest of conserving flora and fauna, and protecting the littoral zone. It also allows more water to be fished and extends the guide's prescription of antidepressants. There comes a point when you have to look after yourself.

When Nature Calls

The whistlers and ringnecks were coming straight into our decoys, and our muzzles were hot even though dawn was but a half hour behind us. It had been a long time since the ducks had been so accommodating. We were watching four blacks circle over Mud Brook looking for companions to feed with, when they spotted our decoys. I could tell they would set their wings at any moment.

Suddenly Andy rose to his feet, straddled the blind, and bolted for the woods. I couldn't believe he would pick this moment to relieve himself, and neither could his yellow Lab, Samantha. The blacks veered and went their merry way.

A few minutes later I heard a shout from the alders nearby. "Dale, did you bring any toilet paper with you?"

Two ringnecks cupped their wings and lit into the outside decoys. Don't move, I told myself.

"Hey! Do we have any newspaper out there in the blind?"

The drake was restless and quacked twice, the way they do when something's not right. I hunkered down and Sam did likewise, the only sounds coming from our breathing.

"Yo, Dale! Have you got change for a twenty?"

The two ducks took to the air, and I could have sworn that drake had a sheepish grin on his face. Sam sighed.

It occurred to me then, and since, that getting "caught short" can be one of life's darkest moments. But despite its inconvenience, this situation need not be uncomfortable or undignified.

Guides learn early about life's timing problems and have developed singular skills to accommodate such moments. Although a few guides view these talents as professional secrets and part of their mystique, I believe that others trapped in the same predicament, in haste and unable to postpone, can benefit from their knowledge. Therefore, at risk of excommunication I will disclose some inside information.

One cautionary note is in order. If you must choose a site having a sharp incline, always face uphill. Enough said.

As a matter of convention, most people are familiar with what we'll call Position A, whereby the participant is seated over a fallen log. This method has a long and revered tradition. As time is often critical, the user should not be overly selective of height, but matters of size and species are particularly relevant. Small logs cannot support the weight of large persons, but logs too large in diameter can introduce problems of deflection. Hardwoods usually do not have the bark scales of conifers and therefore are favored for  reasons of comfort. Some guides like a covering of moss. In all events, the contact area should be scrutinized for stubbly branches. One advantage of Position A is that it frees both hands to ward off mosquitoes.

Position B involves the use of a "gripper," usually a small sapling which the user faces and grasps with either one or both hands. Some of the boys like a golf grip but I prefer the baseball grip, which permits one to choke up on the sapling to apply differentials in pressure. Two factors are critical in the selection of a gripper: first, the sapling should be green to afford strength, and second, the tree should be well rooted. Bushes having thorns are less desirable.

The backrest method (Position C) is popular among veteran outdoorsmen and has much to commend it. The person firmly plants both feet, then gently leans back until the back braces squarely against a tree trunk. The need for secure footing cannot be overemphasized.

When selecting an appropriate tree to use as a backrest, care should be taken that the tree does not angle backward. This is not simply a matter of good posture. Any tree that

angles backward above the user must angle forward below the user, and this can disrupt the normal path of gravity.

The backrest method is good for strengthening the quadriceps, but should not be chosen if one has no quadriceps to begin with. Besides providing good support for the spine, the technique also frees both hands for fly patrol. A hearty push is needed when the project is complete.

The terrain may prompt one to choose Position D, whereby the subject makes use of virtually any high object as a "leaner." Boulders, stumps, blowdowns, or hummocks will suffice. Duck hunters sometimes use a Lab or Chesapeake. Keeping the object immediately to one's side, the subject transfers his or her weight to the support with an arm or with direct contact to the body. Ex-football players use the straight-arm method, which works well if the elbow locks properly.

Users of this method should place the support object on their left if they are right-handed, and vice versa.

Finally, the free-standing method (Position E) should never be overlooked. As an emergency maneuver it has won many subscribers over the years and, although not fancy or trendy, has a broad base of appeal. Being non-site-specific, the technique can be implemented with speed.

During fly season one should choose high ground whenever possible, or the occasion will be distasteful regardless of accomplishment. If every mosquito in the county is in attendance and if the mechanics involve longer operational time than planned, it is wise to duck-walk twenty paces and resume operation.

I recall having tissue paper with me once. It was in 1974. At times when you need to substitute I can suggest your handkerchief, leaves, moss, birchbark, the canoe sponge, a sock, the tail of your shirt (torn off), or a credit-card invoice. Rex used to use the credit card itself.

Better substitutes are available to the resourceful. One small napkin or piece of facial tissue can be carefully torn into small strips, each strip then wrapped around a handful of moss or leaves. The resulting product has bulk and a soft exterior, the essential properties of the real thing. Newspaper is about as good as a dry pine cone, but can become both soft and effective if dunked in a nearby lake or stream prior to use. Heck, they're even selling stuff like that now at the drug counters.

Hopefully, these remarks will be useful to some readers when confronting the process of elimination. Just in case, however, carry some small bills with you.

Distinguishing Little Fish from Big Fish

O ne evening on the Allagash, Clarence Jalbert was frying up a mess of brook trout for his party. The local warden was motoring upstream in his canoe when he noticed the campfire and came ashore for some company.

"Got the pot on, Clarence?"

"Grab a cup and help yourself, Frank."

The warden poured himself some coffee, rubbed his hands beside the fire, and stood up. His eyes immediately fell on the thirty-seven brookies huddled together in the sizzle.

"Pretty small trout, weren't they, Clarence?" asked the warden.

"Not really, Frank. Got these where Miles Brook comes in. I don't know why, but the trout around there have awfully long heads."

The distinguishing features between little fish and big fish are subtle and usually have nothing to do with size. This is why guides prefer to speak in terms of *nice* fish and *good* fish.

Proportions are defined by social, not biological criteria. This explains why 97.3 percent of all game species qualify as good fish or nice fish, the residual being trophy fish or fry. The social magnitude of each fish is determined by such criteria as when and where it was caught, who caught it, what happened to it, and who is listening.

Among guides, a nice fish is heftier, on average, than a good fish. It all has to do with relativity. A *nice* fish is one that compares favorably with the moving average over the last several years. A *good* fish is one that compares favorably with the moving average over the last couple of hours. This means that a bass can fall into a broad range of weights and lengths and still qualify as a good bass, depending upon the day and the waters being fished.

For example, the criterion for a good fish diminishes significantly in the hour before lunch. Any fish that is designated for the grill or frypan is a good fish by consensus. If it is fully consumed, it immediately qualifies as a nice fish.

Missing a nice fish tends to broaden one's vocabulary. Losing a good fish is not as expansive linguistically, but does reacquaint the angler with many old terms not used since adolescence.

A guide wants a nice fish to jump before it gets off. This way everyone has a chance to appreciate the size. Whether it jumps or not, you lose the fish. But if you don't *see* it, you lose the story as well. Everyone is better off if the good fish don't jump.

It bears mention that should a fish be declared a nice fish by the sport, by convention the guide will defer to the sport's better judgment. Sports are generally less competent in identifying small fish, hence the guide's judgment is sometimes needed. Under Maine statute the guide's decision is final.

It is fashionable for people to fish with ultralight gear, which is okay so long as they are catching fish in the diminutive range. Any fish caught on ultralight, for all intents and purposes, is at least a good fish. But about the time a nice fish comes along and is lost because the rod didn't have enough backbone to stick him properly, it is time to change to a stiffer outfit. Sports never appreciate it when the guide uses their light rod as a colonoscope.

Somehow nearly all the fish caught in the good old

days were long and hefty. Nobody can ever remember when the flies were thicker than they are this year. No one can recall seeing the wind blow harder, the alders thicker, or the stream level lower. But the fish were always bigger years ago. I am

always grateful when a client tells me how small the fish are compared to what he used to catch in the little pond behind his house. I especially enjoy the old photos of huge stringers of bass, which he carted around the neighborhood until the odor caused a public complaint.

Bass and trout experience their greatest rate of growth in the memories of the people who caught them. If hatchery biologists could provide similar nutrition for reared fish, the stocking truck would be full of wall-hangers.

Perhaps the greatest distortion regarding fish size has to do with photography. A person's arm elongates by as much as fifty percent whenever someone offers to take a picture of his fish, with the coefficient of expansion directly proportional to the experience of the angler. Some veteran fishermen are able to stretch their arms enough to change the light bulbs in a high-school gym without using a ladder. Only photographs of small children with their catches hold any validity. The rest are fishy.

Very few anglers carry an accurate set of scales with them. I used to think it had to do with price, but I now realize that few people *want* anything that is precise.

Although big fish and little fish resist cardinal definition, they are relatively easy to rank ordinally. Even guides are able to tell which fish is bigger when two are held side by side. For this reason it is nice to have everyone else reel in when a decent fish is being played. This way the fish cannot compare unfavorably and, once released, is as big as any of the others.

"Big fish are better than little fish; little fish are better than no fish; and something is better than nothing." These words many times my father said. Three pickerel are better than no bass. Ten chub are better than no trout. Six white perch are better than no salmon. Just ask anyone who is paid to find fish.

Guides who are competent at distinguishing good fish from fry generally bring a couple fish in for lunch. Guides without this capability usually bring in a handful of fillets. The other guides know what the deal is.

My friend Dan Bean, also known as "Big Dan," told me

that you can get a short landlock to attain legal length and thus make him eligible for the broiler simply by standing on the fish for a few moments. I have attempted this several times with little success other than to slime up my boots and void the salmon's candidacy for release. Big Dan's consistency at this trick may have something to do with his 338 pounds, but I have never inquired.

Outdoor media people often have difficulty in distinguishing respectable fish from fingerlings. Since they already know the weight of each species necessary to sell magazines, why do they even bother to go fishing? Why not just write the story and to hell with the trip? Hunting editors would never stoop to shoot a doe unless, of course, there was a need for "camp meat."

Assessing a fish is best accomplished by comparing him with the angler's expectations, assuming the sport did not come armed with magazine articles. When one's expectations are reasonable it is hard to come back disappointed. A little sense of perspective can help guides endure years at their occupation.

It's worth repeating that a fish's proportions are much easier to determine if the fish is lost rather than caught. After all, the little one never got away.

Knots

There are two kinds of knots—intentional and unintentional. The clinch knot and blood knot are of the former variety; wind knots and backlashes are of the latter. Intentional knots sometimes hold; unintentional knots always hold.

Good clinch knots are taken for granted. Bad ones are usually blamed on the guide. Guides learn this early on. Since a guide is ultimately responsible for the bad knots he didn't even tie, and because he suffers more disappointment than anyone else when a knot slips, he figures he might as well tie them himself. Upon landing a big fish no one ever turns to the guide and remarks on what a splendid knot he tied.

Every now and then somebody, in the winter boredom of his living room, invents a new knot with which to attach a fishing lure. Thus we see Palomar knots and overhand loops and uni-knots and modified figure-eights and resurrected double clinches with somebody's name attached to it. When modern extrusion produced monofilament that is smooth and uniform in diameter, the original clinch knot became inadequate. But the extra loop in the improved clinch knot took care of that thirty years ago. All the other knots were devised to occupy those periods between bites on a lazy summer afternoon, or because someone felt the Boy Scout Handbook was not long enough.

Ford Brooks, a young man who guided in the early 1980s to help pay for college, developed an interesting knot that he used to tie his canoe to the trailer. The knot had the special properties of being unable to hold anything securely, always generating four inches of slack line, but would not permit itself to be untied. Ford is now a clinical psychologist in Richmond, Virginia.

Much more can be said about unintentional knots. In fact, much more generally is said about them.

Fly-fishing brings a special dimension to the word "tangle." Even veteran fly-fishers marvel at their own creativity. Anyone who has fly-fished over ten years can be credited with at least six original knots never observed by the rest of the human race. Unfortunately, most of these knots have no further application.

Slack line off the fly reel will insidiously catch every conceivable object in its path, and many inconceivable objects as well. This has provided tackle manufacturers with exciting new applications for their products. Given their superior snagging properties, professional wranglers recently switched to size-ten or size-twelve weight-forward floating lines to retrieve errant steers. Backcasts were the stimulus for modern weedwhackers and explain why the Orvis casting pools are so free of obstructions: the brush has simply been mowed down.

Some of the most fascinating knots are the ones that appear in the anchor lines of rental boats at the lodge. I don't believe they could be duplicated, even with good illustrations. The ones that show up in decoy lines are also beauties. I've often wanted to take some of these into a major airport somewhere to give people something to do while they wait for their flights.

Snarls and tangles do not properly qualify as knots, at least at first, but they eventually become knots. The incidence of these messes can be predicted using Solunar Tables; that is, they occur about the time the fish start biting. *The size of a backlash is always directly proportional to the size of the fish you raised on your last cast.* The nature of the ensuing mess depends mainly on your fishing style.

It all boils down to one's propensity to create slack at just the wrong moment. If you are fly-casting, the fly line drops in coils around your body. If you are fishing a dry fly, it winds up buried in the mesh of your shirt, whereas a wet fly or streamer manages to settle under a rock and is snagged by the time you get your act together. If you are spin-fishing with a plug, it could have wound up most anywhere. And if you are using one of those fancy bait-casters, you know damned well what happened. While you fight your way through bundles of concertina wire, your buddy hooks *your* fish.

In New England we use a variety of tandem-hook streamers for landlocked salmon. These blow around in the wind like other flies and ultimately wind up stuck in the back of your collar or jacket. The neat thing about them is that when you try to get the trail hook out of your collar, the lead hook somehow catches your sleeve. Then you're in a pickle.

If, by some act of Providence, you manage to tie into a decent fish, you are still not home free. Guides usually find that about the time they are ready to dip a big salmon, the other fellow has dangled his nine-hook Rapala into the net. Or else it was a Flatfish.

It's sometimes better just to fish alone.

Rods rigged with tackle should never be placed together unless you are truly bored for something to do. In fact, you can set these rods at opposite ends of a warehouse and they will be married within ten minutes. Sports always meet their guide in the morning with every rod bundled together in one hand and their tackle box in the other, a neat way to entertain the guide for an extra ten minutes.

The fishing community has been hoodwinked into buying products that promise to reduce snags and snarls, but which in fact merely perpetuate a long tradition. For example, who is the bright individual who thought up single-footed rod guides? Monofilament will form several half-hitches around single-footed guides without provocation, whereas it used to be a virtual impossibility.

Skirted reel spools were supposed to deter line from getting under the spool and around the reel shaft. Lead-core lines

"HEY! MR. OUTDOORS... I THINK
=THE NAILS COME OUT!"

were to be the tangle-free alternative to Monel and braided brass. Level-winds were intended to eliminate line pile-ups on bait-casting and trolling reels. Right.

I love the little plastic line keepers they put on the sides of open-face spools to hold the tag end of your monofilament. You can't cram the line into the tiny holder, but it protrudes far enough to snag every third cast. A good set of lineman's pliers is the best solution for these bad boys.

The biggest villains among manufacturers, responsible for more lost fishing time than all other equipment failures put together, are the line makers. Some brands of monofilament simply refuse to lie on an open spool. Instead, the coils pop off out of sequence during casts, get caught in the shooting line, and immediately create a bird's nest nonpareil. And the poor angler thinks he did something wrong. Instead of better lines we get a dazzling array of cofilaments and other lines, which also refuse to lie on the spool. Nothing increases line sales like faulty lines.

One June I was fishing with Jerome Robinson, who was then writing for *Sports Afield.* He wanted to get some shots of a guide paddling along the shore with his sports casting, so I nudged up to Rex Boyd's canoe. His bow man was so disgustedly tangled in line that we eventually decided to go fry some fish. Had the man fallen overboard, there would have been no hope. We didn't bother with the photos.

Much in the way of foul-ups is, of course, preventable. Improper techniques and novice error account for more than a few tangles. From the stern seat you can see most tangles during gestation. You risk offending the client by pointing out potential problems, but you can also save yourself a lot of anguish.

Many sports seem to think guides have an affection for snarls and tangles and that we enjoy picking them. Why else would they pass all those Gordian knots to us for inspection and remedy? It usually happens about the time you are negotiating a set of rips, or threading your way through a minefield of boulders, or replacing the needle valve in the carburetor on your motor.

If they passed their rod before they worked on the problem themselves it wouldn't be so bad. Instead, they reel everything up as tight as possible. They pull the line instead of the loops. Or, if their lure is caught in the line itself, they shake it a few dozen times before handing it over. Hell, a few more shakes and they'd have an Irish knit sweater.

Bait-casting reels should have been banned years ago, alongside Chesapeake long guns, gill nets, and jack lights. They have induced many guides to change profession, and caused pain and suffering among those who remained. And overloading a spool on an open-face spinning reel should be a Class A felony.

Keeping
Your Senses

F ord Brooks fished at the lodge with his father each June as
a boy and, upon graduating from high school, expressed
an interest in guiding. Ford grew up in suburban Pennsylvania and, unlike Maine lads, had not spent his youth
catching frogs, tying flies, and trapping "mushrats." But he
was determined to try it, and successfully passed the Maine
Guide exam. He guided a couple of seasons and did fine, making up for his lack of experience with persistence and effort.
Ford is intelligent, conversant, and accommodating, which
goes a long way.

Ford never learned to tie a decent rope knot. Despite our
many efforts to instruct him on bowlines, hitches, and tie-
downs, his creations inevitably created slack line and led to
more than a few close calls. He was using a spare guide canoe
of mine, and that caused some anxiety on my part. His axe-
manship was also weak, and we were afraid he might just kill
himself someday getting his firewood. We could never decide
whether to put a keen edge on his axe or leave it dull as a hoe.
It remained dull—and it got duller.

Andy and I often poked fun at Ford's knots, but in retrospect, we didn't factor in his handicap. Ford was missing the end of his left thumb, and that undoubtedly lessened his dexterity, particularly on cold days. Thumbs are handy for tying knots.

When any young man starts out in the guide profession the lodge owner tries to work him in gently, at first assigning him to large parties in tandem with a seasoned guide. The veteran serves as a mentor while the rookie observes good methods in boatmanship, cooking, and client relations. The older guide's experience and judgment are important for the safety and welfare of the party. Eventually the younger man gains some competence in his own right and develops rapport with his sports, at which time he starts to guide his own parties.

In the spring of 1981, Ford was just getting his feet wet. He had his guide's license and was beginning to pick up practical experience. When two couples arrived at the lodge in late May, I assigned Ford to work in the party alongside my father, Woodie.

The party consisted of two young doctors who were about to confront major marital problems at home, although they were unaware of it at the time. Their fishing partners were two wonderful physical specimens of the fair gender, whose surnames differed from those of the doctors. The men had requested cabins with double beds, the fishing being a diversionary part of the trip. We could see that the gals were not into matching the hatch, but that is not to say their equipment was deficient. This is not something we see a lot of, but, whatever.

The weather was horrendous that May. Day after day, the wind blew from the south, keeping a damp chill in the air whenever it was not raining outright. I was guiding two gentlemen on Spednic Lake this particular day, and the mist had turned to a steady rain soon after we left the landing. By ten, the cold had crept inside every layer of clothing, and by late morning we were all frozen stiff. I decided to seek refuge in a rustic camp my Dad had built for deer hunters years ago, and to which we had a key. We used the camp only when conditions were unbearable, but this day qualified.

Rounding the point by Mud Cove, it was obvious my father had the same idea. He and Ford arrived just ahead of me, and Dad waved me in to join them. The doctors were soaked to the skin and shivering, as were their friends, proper raingear having been somehow overlooked in the haste of their trip planning. Ford was blue, his hands shaking from the cold. We all hurried up the path to the cabin and went in, and I immediately started a fire in the woodstove.

"Camp Ruffit" is a typical one-room affair. The sleeping end has bunk beds near the woodstove, while the other end is the kitchen area. Propane gas from a cylinder out back serves a cookstove and several mounted gas lamps, located so as to aid the cooking and eating (and the nightly poker game). The lighting is not great, but adequate once your eyes get adjusted. Twenty yards behind the camp is the traditional two-holer.

We lit the lamps, primed the water pump, and got settled in. As the fire took hold, the sports huddled over the stove, then began stripping down, hanging their wet clothes on the nails overhead. In the kitchen area, Dad started filleting the few fish we had managed to save for lunch, while Ford and I began to peel the potatoes and onions.

Nothing I have described to this point makes the story unusual. We were all cold and wet. But perhaps we underestimated the physical discomfort of the young ladies. In any event, their method of thawing out we found somewhat unconventional.

My sports were rubbing their hands and making small talk while watching my father clean fish, not standing over by the heat, and I wondered why. Glancing over at the stove area, I noticed that each gal was clad in a wet tee shirt. Period. Now, *maybe* they had panties on. It was pretty hard to tell in the dark of the cabin, and I didn't feel compelled to walk over and check, but it sure didn't look like they were wearing anything down below. The wet top, given the nature of what was underneath, was enough to hold a man's curiosity.

Without being real obvious about it, I elbowed Ford in the ribs and gestured for him to take note. He didn't understand right away, but eventually was able to focus his eyes on

the dim area over by the wood-stove. His furtive interest confirmed my own observations, and his potato peels began to get thicker and thicker. Dad winked. It was right about then that Ford cut off the end of his thumb.

He wasn't much use to us cooking lunch that day, and it's probably all my fault. You can probably blame me for all his lousy. knots, too. But it was worth it.

Attire

Although guides are known to wear some rather unusual clothes, there are a few articles you would not see them caught dead in. For example, you won't see a guide decked out in Pringlehoffer's six-ply, puffin-down, poly-thermolate, Pond-Pruf packing suit. If he is cold, he simply puts on another shirt.

Guides prefer not to wear camouflage in public places. It's hard enough to fool a black duck when you're crouched in a blind, so it makes little sense to try to be invisible at the mall. A guide is conspicuous anyway, particularly among earthlings. He also recognizes bad taste.

Most of us aren't big on embroidered patches, although some guides will use their Registered Maine Guide patch to cover over a nasty tear. Guides do not have an identity problem and would prefer not to look like court jesters. Blaze orange looks fine in the woods but is normally left home during weddings. Rhinestones and G-strings are out.

All guides wear long johns. But these are not considered to be clothing as much as *habitat*.

Exterior clothes consist of multiple layers of worn, tattered shirts and threadbare trousers, full of three-cornered rips and hook holes, all of which have little to do with comfort. Guide attire is designed to provide good ventilation, discourage borrowing, and to stimulate clients into giving tips out of compassion.

One evening as Mitch started to winch his canoe onto the trailer at Baskahegan, the woman he was fishing with let out a gasp. The seat of his trousers was full of gaping holes, exposing bare skin everywhere.

"Why don't you have the decency to cover your rear end in public?" she scolded.

"I'm sorry, ma'am," Mitch replied as he kept on cranking, "but you see, these pants were almost new this morning. I've slid back and forth across the stern seat all day long to counter your weight when you were shifting around and gawking over the gunwale. I've not only worn out my pants, I've got enough splinters in my butt to cook your lunch tomorrow!"

This is not to say guides don't own any of the fancy duds. It is simply that they save them for the off-season, when the hazards of guiding are less damaging to the gear. A fishing guide puts on his good stuff at the beginning of duck season. A deer guide saves his goose-down parka to dress up for a winter outing with the Missus. This explains why sports never see their guide wearing the expensive clothes they bought him.

Pete Pipines and I were hunting Canada geese in Delaware with Ray DeLaurentis. Ray fishes with us in Maine, and he invited us down late one fall on kind of a busman's holiday. I forgot to take my heavy coat, but, thankfully, Pete had brought along a new down parka as an extra. He's much wiser than I am in that regard.

We were hunkered in a pit blind the first morning with about six geese laid out on the ledge behind us, a testimony to the fact that Ray must have been on his gun that day. Suddenly, an old gander came to his senses behind me and wanted out. I thumped his head several times on the side of the blind to put him out of his misery.

"Be careful," remarked Ray, "you're getting blood all over your new coat."

"It's okay," I said. "This is Pete's coat."

Fishing guides often find themselves in the path of misdirected casts. Although we use evasive tactics, it happens anyway. I've seen John Gaskins dance around like a kid at a heavy-metal concert. Andy Brooks will pick and roll, then run a buttonhook pattern past the middle seat, no easy task in a canoe three feet wide. Some men hide in terror below the gunwales until their sports have finished the false casting before poking their heads up. These ploys only work occasionally. The guide just happens to be a convenient target. It is the only trophy category not included in IFGA records.

Although it's hard on the clothes, getting a set of trebles out of your shirt sleeve beats getting it out of your hide. Believe me, there's nothing like having your ear lobe catch the second stage of a double-haul. It's scary enough to have a Montecruz snapped from your lips by a hundred-mile-an-hour popping bug, a technique Bill Reed demonstrated for me one June morning in Patterson Cove. (Bill said I should stop smoking.) Shirts are a guide's first line of self-defense.

I read the other day that guides allocate so much of their income to life and casualty insurance, they have little left to report on Form 1040. According to records filed with the Internal Revenue Service, the beneficiaries on these policies have names like "Barney" or "Rover."

A lady once cast a jointed Pikey Minnow that circled twice around my father's head, eventually fetching up in the front pocket of his flannel shirt. A minute passed, and the Old Man continued to paddle as her husband fished.

"Aren't you going to give my lure back?" queried the woman.

"No," my father responded, "it's a damn sight safer right where it is."

Northern bass guides now wear motorcycle helmets. Made of high-density polymers, these helmets are resilient enough to deflect the heaviest of jointed plugs and lead-head jigs, and the convex shape resists most flies on the backcast. In the era of castaholics, bass pro wannabes, neo-fly fishermen, once-a-year flailers, thrashmasters, and post-retirement fishing wives, they are a necessity. Deer guides can order them in Kevlar.

It is therefore with considerable sheepishness that I describe a recent trip my wife and I took to the Bahamas. It was wintertime, and I had a hankering to catch a bonefish.

On the first morning, we were fishing with a native Bahamian guide named Will Rolle. The tide was in, and I was fly-casting from the bow until the water got low enough to wade

the flats. Will poled the boat around a little mangrove island as we looked for fish, and I was pushing out a little more fly line than I was comfortable with. Pretty soon my forward cast came to a halt and I turned around to see my Crazy Charlie fetched up in Will's cap.

"What you do that for, Mon?" he asked.

"Just getting even, Will," I explained.

He scowled, and I could tell he was trying to remember whether he had ever fished with me before. Damn fool should have ducked.

Many guides carry a large red bandanna to wipe their noses and get the fly dope and sunscreen out of their eyes. You can apply sunscreen to any part of the body, and it will somehow migrate to your eyes in less than five minutes. Those of us who never remember the bandanna just use our sleeves.

Footwear is selected carefully each day on the basis of what the sport is *not* wearing. If the clients are wearing low-cut shoes, the guide puts on his high boots; if the clients are wearing waders, the guide dons sneakers. This is because the height of the sports' boots is always inversely proportional to the distance you have to drag the bow of the canoe to get them to shore. If they cannot easily reach shore with dry feet, you need your high boots; if they can, you don't.

We still wear the L. L. Bean hunting boots, leather tops and rubber bottoms, like our fathers before us. Tree-climbing spikes, so useful for retrieving lures high in the branches, have to be ordered elsewhere. If you have the spikes, you can leave the chainsaw home.

More good money is wasted on waders than on any other wearable gear. Every angler knows that waders are never as high as the water is deep, particularly within casting range of the rise. God made holding pools in two sizes only: Salmon pools are a quarter inch deeper than chest waders; trout pools are a quarter inch deeper than hip waders. It's a lot easier just to get soaked and not have to lug an extra ten gallons of water around.

All rain pants leak, initially in the crotch, and thereafter the location is academic. Manufacturers insist on sewing pockets on raincoats. Nobody ever uses these pockets, and they invariably allow water to infiltrate an otherwise serviceable suit.

The rainshirts traditionally worn by guides Down East are full-length, one-piece garments appropriate for sitting in the rain. They eventually get as wet on the inside from perspiration as on the outside from precipitation, but can be put on or taken off quickly. These garments have to be retrofitted with a ventilator turbine near the shoulder. Since they employ elastic wrist bands, flatulence has a tendency to rise and escape through the head hole, much to the distress of the user.

It's nice to read about all the snazzy clothes available for outdoors people nowadays. During the winter, guides heat their homes with the mail-order catalogs they receive from outdoor-clothing suppliers.

Finding Things Lost

Anyone knows that you find whatever it is you are looking for in the last place you look. But few of us care to consider how stupid we were to lose it in the first place, how much time we wasted trying to locate it, or the utterly ridiculous places we searched in the hope that just maybe it was there.

Experienced guides are masters at finding lost articles, a skill surpassed only by their propensity to lose things in the first place. The net benefit of this differential is that there is less to lug home.

When in the presence of clients, the guide should identify and classify missing items as soon as possible in order to develop a strategy that will save face. Articles should be immediately reported as stolen, borrowed, or apprehended whenever possible, since this implicates the other guides, the lodge owner, or the warden and diverts suspicion from the guide. Only as a last resort should items be pronounced lost, misplaced, or forgotten. Since the guide's reputation is at stake, his prudent selection of adjectives to describe missing articles can go a long way toward damage control.

Confessing that something is "lost" is not ignoble, and may even produce benefits. All sportsmen and sportswomen can relate to the predicament. Thus, a public display of disgust, punctuated with a liberal dose of expletives, helps the bonding process. Astute guides will sometimes refer to missing gear as lost when they do not even own the equipment in the first place (but should), or else it has been broken since last year and they haven't gotten around to fixing it.

Certain important items cannot be convincingly reported as lost or misplaced, and aspiring guides should be aware of this. For example, hunters find it implausible that the guide misplaced his firearm. Similarly, fishermen find it difficult to believe that a guide would "lose" the lunch, the bait, or his outboard motor. Since the drive back to camp is twice as far when you forget items of this magnitude, and because it is hard to shift the blame, a guide must learn to identify the things he forgot as soon as possible. There is rarely enough gas in the truck to make more than one such mistake on any given day.

The size and nature of a lost article often provide clues as to where to search. Unfortunately, most people make the mistake of concentrating their efforts in likely spots when they could save much time by going directly to the places where things generally turn up. For example, anything smaller than a horse is likely to be in last fall's hunting vest. In boats, the first place an angler should look for anything is under the gas can. Many sportsmen carry their life possessions stuck in their hat, so this is a good place to try. At home, check which drawer your wife shoves the contents of your pockets when she does the wash.

Never bother to look for tent pegs, since these are always lost, and you're bound to find plenty at the next campsite anyway. You shouldn't try too hard to find something you lost trout fishing either, unless you can remember *exactly* where it was that nature called.

Dan Bean once lost a dozen white perch he had saved to take home for supper. It wasn't until a week later, during a cold snap, that they were located. It seems that he was on his way to one of the outlying lakes when the lady he was guiding complained of a certain fragrance. Dan didn't notice it, but agreed to look around anyway. There, stuck under the heater in the pickup, were the perch. They were all wrapped up in Dan's union suit.

Losing something in a confined area, such as your canoe or tackle box or fly book or pocket, can be particularly embarrassing. Knowing that the item absolutely, positively has to be in a certain location obstructs the search by narrowing the focus area, generally resulting in a longer recovery time. Tackle boxes, for example, are not subject to any systematic filing

methods, yet aggressively consume everything around them. You are about as likely to find the Holy Grail as anything placed in your box.

Consider lures. Sports mistakenly assume that fishing lures are inanimate objects and therefore immobile. On the contrary, only the ineffective baits stay put. Any decent lure placed in your tackle box immediately hops from tray to tray, slithers into the biggest pile of debris it can find, and burrows beneath. If you are lucky, it avoids the tray where the rubber worms are all fused together with the plastic containers. Meanwhile, all those lures that wouldn't snag a fish in a hatchery pool sit proudly in their bright finishes without moving a muscle from year to year.

The expression "terminal tackle" implies life, albeit brief. The term has nothing to do with its position on the end of a line but, rather, to its life expectancy. Effective baits are soon lost to fish, to the propeller, or to the bowels of your tackle box, never to resurface until the hooks are rusted off and the colors faded. Nothing has a shorter life expectancy than your hottest salmon fly. Lousy lures last forever.

There are a number of techniques for recovering lost lures from a tackle box. The best method is to dredge directly into the bottom hold. First, remove the extra reel, sunglasses, spools of line, and larger items. These are easy to identify because they are the only dry items in the box. Next take out the lure boxes, fly dope, and De-Liar that is so corroded that the tape no longer pulls out. Slide the bobbers and fish scent to one side so your buddy won't know you use them. Now dig through the pliers and screwdrivers, go underneath the togue spoons you have saved for twenty years but never use, until you see a miscellany of used split shot and rusty hooks of all sizes. Finally you will reach the *gunk,* a brown composting mass of suntan lotion, citronella, reel lube, perch scales, and brine that leaked from the pork-rind jar. You won't find what you are looking for here, but in the process you will discover at least two items you misplaced the last day you went fishing.

The digging method turns up many things you forgot you had. From my tackle box I have excavated such items as a set of antlers from an eight-point I shot in high school, several dog biscuits, an extra set of long johns, and my grandfather's anvil.

An alternative approach is to wave the bag of your dip net over the top shelf of your tackle box. This is often done inadvertently as you prepare to net a nice salmon. The net gathers up seventeen streamers, six Mepps spinners, nine Rapalas, and three lead-head jigs, on average, all of which are displayed for ready identification. By the way, if your sport does have a salmon on, tell him the fish is not ready and should be played for another hour.

You can also use the "macro" method, popular among sports who wish to assist the guide. This involves emptying the entire contents of the box on the floor of the canoe, simplifying the search considerably. Clients always do this when they help the guide unload his canoe at the end of the day, grabbing his box without ever checking to see if it is latched. Unfortunately, this procedure is regularly used even when the guide is not looking for anything.

Several recovery methods will not be recommended here, despite their proven effectiveness. Sitting down in a boat or canoe without carefully inspecting your seat is bound to turn up something with hooks on it. It is also best not to let fifty feet of anchor rope slide through your fingers unrestrained, as somewhere in the rope lies that lure you've been looking for. Those who insist on this technique might want to consider a light anchor.

The thrill of serendipity occurs whenever a guide finds items that belong to his client, discovered long after the fellow has gone home and which are not expensive enough to send him. Guides keep themselves resupplied in this manner. The floor behind the seat of a pickup truck is a treasure trove at the end of the season, and explains why no guide has ever purchased a new compass or whetstone. Few guides are overly thorough when they empty their canoes on the last day of a party's stay, since many good things show up here. In fact, some guides go so far as to use a canoe-length carpet runner to conceal small objects that slip down between the ribs. The booty found in these places helps to compensate the guide for all the tackle his sports lose.

Misplacing a hot fly causes severe anguish among trout and salmon guides. Salmon guides stick streamers in the side ribs of their canoe as they work through them until upwards of fifty flies are displayed, none of which have attracted a sniff. They give a professional appearance to the stern as well as a sense of progress to the guide but, more importantly, leave fewer flies in the book to confuse with his two good ones.

Losing one's jackknife is the ultimate cause of concern, as it is the most essential and versatile tool a guide carries. He uses it to cut bait, to remove the guts from a pickerel, to scrape yesterday's meat from the broiler, and to surgically remove hooks from the sports. Furthermore, a guide can survive two to three weeks in the wild on the organic material wedged in his jackknife. If you lose your knife, good luck.

Submerged Hazards

A ll guides strike rocks from time to time. The better guides tend to be traveling slower when they hit them.

George MacArthur, an old waterman from Grand Lake Stream, was guiding a New York couple on Big Lake.

"By now I'll bet you know every rock in this lake," offered the woman.

About that time the bow lifted as a nasty bulge rippled its way to the stern, ending with a clunk and the grinding sound of metal blades on granite. The small outboard lurched forward, sending spray in every direction, and finally settled back into position.

"Yup," said George, "there's one right there."

Unfortunately, when you do hit a rock it is usually the one you meant to fish. Nothing sends a smallmouth into a feeding frenzy like the jolt of a lower unit crashing into his bedroom.

The problem is that underwater hazards are migratory, something sports fail to appreciate. Submerged rocks always relocate in foggy weather. The rock piles in Spednic Lake migrate several hundred yards from year to year but never wind up where you expect them. Shoals shift with wind conditions, but not predictably. Bars protrude at whim. Dead-head logs move surreptitiously in the night to appear at different spots on consecutive days, and will sometimes reach up and tunk the bottom of your canoe when you are lying still in the water, wholly innocent.

Scientists have long studied the phenomenon. They have correlated the timing of collisions with certain environmental disturbances, but do not understand causation. Researchers know, for example, that guides tend to strike more obstacles during lake drawdowns, on turbid waters, during heavy glare, during the blackfly season, and when they are in a hurry to get somewhere. The *reasons* for the sudden shift in bedrock, however, have not been documented.

Structure tends to remain relatively stable whenever the bow man is sitting down, when he is not putting on his raincoat, and when he weighs less than three hundred pounds.

Under these conditions, waters can be charted with relative accuracy and traversed safely.

Drake Lake, near the village of Brookton, was the recent subject of a government study on seismic shift. The water in Drake Lake is dark brown in color, a result of the abundant humic material in the basin and a slow flushing rate. It is so dark that you cannot see the blade of your paddle on a stroke. The native bass grow to great size without ever finding the outlet and have bruised heads from running into granite ledges and unseen outcroppings of shale. Even electronic soundings from the transducer get lost before returning to the boat. Geologists have been working with local guides to learn why the shallow rocks in the lake move capriciously and frequently smash the motors of guides who are well aware of them. They think it could be due to a fault.

Flowed waters create a different type of problem. Stumps regenerate until they are exactly the level of the lake surface and frequently grab the keel of a Grand Lake canoe at midships. St. Croix Flowage is famous for this. Surrounded by six feet of water, the guide can find nothing upon which to get a purchase, cannot pry against the stump itself since it lies directly underneath, so winds up rotating his twenty-foot craft on its pivot point. Sports take great mirth in this escapade. The guide, too, considers it hilarious.

Tree trunks floating just below the surface can be great fun when you have the motor wide open. This is dri-ki in its larval stage, common just after ice-out and during high water. There's nothing like it to keep you awake at the helm.

Going ashore is also hazardous, not because of the number of obstacles but because they are so unavoidable. Never in modern history has a guide approached shore when the person in the bow did not jump to his feet to prevent the boat from hitting a boulder, thereby blocking the guide's vision and ensuring a collision with that boulder. Half the winter is dedicated to replacing the fiberglass around the stem.

Seasonal cottage owners from away love to mark hazards with Clorox bottles. Guides are always pleased to find a white jug on one of their favorite fishing spots; they really appreciate the decorative touch of polyethylene in God's country. Guides who carry jackknives tend to believe that anyone who goes racing around in a motorboat ought to have an inkling of what is underneath them besides water.

To Ride a Moose

O ne warm July morning in 1979 my brother Lance and I took turns riding a bull moose across the mouth of McAllister Cove, a large arm of Spednic Lake. We didn't do it to be macho or sadistic. Our purpose was wholly academic, and any fun we may have had was coincidental. We wanted to find out if it is possible to ride a swimming moose. It is.

We were prepared. Anyone can jump on a wild beast out of impulse, but it was not like that. Stupidity is a desirable character trait for moose riding, and I had practised it for years. I had also ridden my grandfather's old workhorse once or twice at the age of ten, and therefore was confident of my equestrian skills. Lance had even watched a couple episodes of "Wild Kingdom."

We carefully searched the literature, as in "Moose, riding of; *see also* Bull" and, upon finding nothing, figured there wasn't much to it. We browsed the local tack shops for saddlery they might recommend, made sure we had all the necessary permits, and even went through the L. L. Bean catalog to see if any special footwear was available. In those days you could afford health insurance. We were ready.

Confronting a swimming moose in Maine is relatively common. Finding all the circumstances right to actually get on one is a little trickier, especially if someone has hired you to find them a fish.

First of all, it is important to get the moose far enough into open water that his itinerary does not include dry ground. Although the literature is sadly lacking in the details surrounding conventional moose riding in heavily forested areas, we wished to confine our research to water transport. In fact, we were not about to let his feet strike bottom with one of us aboard, afraid the additional weight could cause injury to the hooves. This attests to our overall concern for the safety of the moose.

Another consideration is water temperature. Maine's climate is not conducive to all-season moose riding, as the lakes can get pretty nippy. Mid-summer is about the only time you would care to tackle it, and then only when there is plenty of sun. Jumping on a moose in cold water may bring a guide's judgment into question. And guiding in a wetsuit tends to distract the client.

You should choose your beast carefully. I'm not talking about a Boone and Crockett candidate or anything like that. The fact is, the folks you are fishing with are more than likely to evaluate your performance, and the improper choice of a steed can reduce overall marks significantly. For example, I considered riding a cow moose one time while her calf bleated from the shore nearby. The day was perfect. The water was deep. But the lady I was guiding started using all these fancy buzzwords, most of which I missed on account of the motor. I did hear things like "perverted," "ASPCA," and "despicable." I could see she was clearly anti-research.

On the subject of clients. While most sports do not share the same enthusiasm for this research topic as does a guide, it is nice if they are supportive. Ideally, your party not only accepts the value of professional inquiry, but will still entertain the notion of paying you at the end of the day. It's also a plus if you have a sport under the age of ninety-three who can quickly absorb the twelve-second crash course in motor operation, can step to the stern without dumping the canoe, and is not likely to head back to the landing the moment you jump on the moose. This may explain why libraries are spotty on the subject.

By the way, Lance and I were guiding separate parties that day, single men with whom we had fished before and who we felt were competent at the controls. Lance was guiding Jim Stoneberger, who owns a large construction company near Boston. I was guiding Ron Hurston, a psychiatrist from Framingham, Massachusetts. My first trip with Ron had been a week of trout fishing and whitewater canoeing on the upper St. John several years earlier. It was on that trip that Ron's portable john collapsed, but that's a different story.

Rounding the end of Hinkley Point, I could see Lance fishing a nearby drop-off. Well beyond him a moose was wading in the shallows off a Canadian bar. Lance's faster motor allowed him to reach the moose first and he was able to wedge his canoe between the moose and shore, forcing the animal to deeper water.

The novelty of watching a moose swim across open water wears off pretty quickly.

"I think I'll try riding him, Ron," I said. "Suppose you can run the motor for a bit?"

Ron looked at me thoughtfully and measured his words. "Have you ever thought about counseling?" he asked.

Shoes off, wallet out, I ran the canoe alongside the animal and leaped straight onto his back. It was my best rendition of Hopalong Cassidy from childhood memory. Lacking reins, I sank my fingers into the long, black hair that covered the hump above his shoulders. The moose was real impressed.

He surged, twisting his head around from time to time to get a better look at me. His antlers were still in velvet and had not reached their full growth, much to his dismay. Even when he craned his neck I was well beyond reach, and he was too busy swimming to devote much time to animosity. That was the plan.

Twice he went below and rolled on his side to force me off. But neither time did he go so deep that I was unable to breathe, and eventually he returned to the surface for air. The first time he did this, I wondered if I was too much burden. He

stayed under a very long time, and I was about ready to jump ship, but it became apparent this was part of his strategy. A moose's lung capacity is enormous, refined by years of feeding on aquatic vegetation.

A solid mass of flies, six inches in diameter, perched on the top of his head. They expressed little interest in me until the moose took his first dive, then decided to get real friendly. The fly looked something like a housefly with shorter wings, and was more nuisance than hazard. The flies wound up following our canoes around the rest of the morning, as a reminder of the responsibilities a ship has toward the passengers of a disabled vessel.

After a while, the moose resigned himself to my presence and straightened out his course for the nearest shore, ears flopping with each stroke. At no time could I determine whether he was a pacer or a trotter. But, having collected enough data to satisfy the inquiry, I returned to the canoe.

My brother then tried his hand at moose riding, and displayed both style and poise. After trying several traditional mounts for comfort and fit, he settled on the old "drag from the stern" technique described on page 183 of *The Field Guide to Modern Moosemanship.* I would say with no exaggeration that Lance is one of the finest moose riders I have ever observed.

Ultimately, we dispatched the moose to the nearest headland. His traction improved markedly when his feet struck bottom, and he wasted little time making the woods. The EPA might have frowned on his departing gesture, directed mainly at Lance and me, but the forest needs nutrients, too.

I can't remember much about the fishing that day. It was sunny, with hardly a breeze. Ron kept asking me how long I had been having this problem and whether I would care to talk to him about it, and other weird questions like that. He would look directly at me, but his eyes seemed to be focused about a foot behind my head. I told him my clothes were drying out, except for my undies.

How Many Fish?

G uides fall into three categories: there are the ones who
can count properly, and the ones who can't. Most are of
the latter ilk. Math incompetency becomes apparent in
Maine lads when they return from their first trout fishing trip
with their "limit" of brookies.

Although many anglers keep a tally of the number of
fish they catch, nothing could be more ridiculous.

For one thing, if the fishing was great, who had time to
count? Whenever people claim to have caught some ungodly
number of game fish, be it bass or whatever, they obviously
did not spend much time playing each fish. And the reason
they didn't was either because the fish were very small or because they horsed them in. Either way, they could not have
stopped long enough to appreciate the day and what they
had.

People are more inclined to count their fish when there
are not too many to count. The day's tally is reported eagerly
to imply a good day. To anyone who has hung around lodges,
it suggests exactly the opposite.

Guides are better off if they never count the number of
fish their parties catch. Ever. Accuracy depends on a good
memory, good math, and honesty—none of which are a guide's
forte. If backed into a corner, a guide should simply wait until

everybody else has spouted a number and then add six. They'll get the message after awhile.

A central problem lies in what to count. For example, only if everyone initially agrees to a particular species of game fish, not something else caught in the course of fishing, of legal size or, better yet, of respectable size (and so defined at the outset), that is hooked properly and *caught* (i.e., boated or netted or touched or from which the hook is manually removed), and caught by someone included in the agreement and confirmed on the basis that that person both set the hook and landed the fish, unless other rules apply, and whether or not the guide's rod is eligible, and regardless of whether the fish was taken or released unharmed, but not to include the same fish twice if caught twice, and each fish weighed on reliable scales by a person not legally blind, *then* people could make honest comparisons. Maybe.

But people count fish in order to make favorable comparisons, not honest ones. Here lies the rub.

It is fashionable, considerate, and correct to release fish. It is also noble. Then again, it is easy to be noble if you weren't brought up on chipped beef on toast.

Catch and release is a philosophy most people practise in reverse order. The majority of game fish are released long before they are caught, some three feet from the boat and some thirty feet from the boat. All of us are familiar with the Palm Beach release, some more intimately than others. Sports often think the choice of verbs, "hooked" versus "caught," is merely a matter of semantics. Guides like to get their grimy paws on a fish to count him caught, and this is perhaps a character flaw.

Catch and release can also be a convenience, especially if a person confuses the two. Take a guy who counts every fish he catches. Of the thirty-four smallmouths he reported to his friend at the end of the day, the hook was only removed from eleven. One rationalization reads, "He was close enough to net if we wanted him." Another is, "I gave him slack so he could get loose." And then there is always, "I was planning to release him anyway." Guides resist any temptation to correct the sport's math, as it becomes part of their own curriculum vitae.

Guides pretend to be honest, but it is a virtue with which they have little exposure or experience. Honesty involves the law of truth. While guides might consciously try to observe the letter of the law, it is the spirit of the law that gives them trouble. My old friend Ralph started out fairly honest, but he got over it.

For example, if a guide expounds on the number of trout his sport "raised," or the number of landlocks they "heard from," or the number of bass his party "hooked," you might get the impression he had a good day. Other guides don't fall for that.

As a guide, you never round off. Instead of "over twenty," it is preferable to say "twenty-nine." Instead of "three pounds," you say "three pounds, one ounce." A very safe answer is, "We released twenty-nine." Revisiting the difficulties associated with definition, you get the picture.

It is preferable to cite the fish you do not kill rather than the ones you do kill. This suggests a sense of ethics. If you follow this line of reasoning, there were a great many fish I did not kill every day I guided.

Among those who count, each day sets a standard for the next. If a sport catches eighteen today, he will be disappointed by seventeen tomorrow. This mentality always tickles the guide.

Counting should take other forms. If you only had one or two lures on all day, you probably had a great day. If you only thought of the office four times today, you had a terrific day. If the guide gave you hell for losing eight consecutive fish, you had a good day. And if you had three helpings at lunch, fine.

One cold May when my folks owned the lodge, the salmon were particularly comatose. One gentleman had fished several days without a strike when he finally tied into a five-pounder. Curious to know what the fish had been feeding on, he took out his jackknife and slit the salmon's stomach. Out popped five smelts.

After two more hours without a strike, the man returned to the lodge where he showed my father his catch, along with the smelts. About that time the phone rang.

"How are they biting, Woodie?"

"Not bad at all. One fellow just now came in with six fish. One of them weighed five pounds."

Buying the Best

A broadly held view among the sporting public is that better, more expensive equipment can substitute for practice and proficiency, providing a shortcut to success in the field. The acquisition of high-performance gear yields an instant competitive advantage over fish and game, otherwise attainable only by learning to use standard gear with more expertise. The philosophy is, of course, valid.

Purchase should be favored over practice whenever feasible. It is a time-honored wisdom deeply rooted in the doctrine of free choice, legitimized by advertising copy, reinforced by peer pressure, and nurtured by our affection for technological progress. Given the severe limits of available time, buying stuff is good judgment.

Accordingly, it is high time someone responded to the subversive elements within our society who would undermine the American addiction to finer equipment and the pursuit of happiness. These morons would argue that we need to develop greater competence in the use of rod and gun, learn more about the ways of quarry, spend more time in the field, and have a better understanding for Nature on her terms.

They forget that working people today have little time for such pursuits and can well afford to avoid the drudgery of more education.

Buying the best generates high levels of expenditures, while promoting incompetence afield. A related phenomenon, the American sportsman's insatiable appetite for more and more outdoor equipment regardless of need, produces similar effects. I don't know of anybody, at least anybody over the age of twelve, who can cram all their outdoor junk under one roof. These tenets of consumer behavior serve many diverse interests for the betterment of society.

First of all, it is now possible to purchase self-esteem. By acquiring merchandise labeled "for the man of distinction" or "for only the discriminating sport and collector who appreciates the tradition of fine craftsmanship" or "designed for the person of pedigree who can recognize superior quality," etc., persons of finite income can now gain immediate access to rank and title without the petty obstacles of legacy or social grace. There is no shorter route to dignity.

Those on a slightly different tack can purchase products offering the advantage of technological breakthrough, high-performance materials, laser-crafted components, and precision assembly. These might include faster-action semi-automatics, reels with high-speed retrieval ratios, and high-resolution big-game satellite surveillance systems. Much pride comes with owning and displaying sophisticated equipment. Fondling it with friends and neighbors while reciting manufacturers' specs is wholesome fun.

Let's face it. The old fishing aristocracy doesn't want us catching big fish on a bunch of cheap crap. A couple years ago the International Game Fish Association disallowed a world-record brown trout caught by some young fellow on the White River in Arkansas. He had gobbed some corn mixture on a tiny treble hook—it was a sixteen or something like that—and hooked the fish off his dock. It took an eternity to land the monster, and it was wholly legal under Arkansas fish and game laws. The IFGA, however, in its infinite wisdom felt the world record should not be caught on a treble hook. This confirms that outfitting oneself with expensive tackle is the only correct approach.

The economy benefits, too. Consumer purchases of sporting goods pump billions of dollars into the U. S. economy each year, contributing significantly to GDP while creating jobs and incomes for millions of people. Economists have estimated that such purchases would decline 93 percent if hunters and anglers purchased only what they needed. Additional

"SO, WHAT'S THE LATEST IN BASS TACKLE? I COULDN'T MAKE IT IN YESTERDAY."

millions are spent each year on sheds and garages to store newly acquired merchandise, and on twin-axle trailers to transport it to the woods.

Equipment used in the wild used to be chosen for its utility, versatility, and durability. The Department of Commerce has determined that each of these properties is harmful to the manufacturing base. Industry leaders have cooperated fully by designing special-purpose products of dubious merit that wear out on the eighth day of use and cannot be repaired. It is called market segmentation and is admired by our trade partners overseas.

On the supply side, less time allocated for hands-on use of gear has meant more time for developing job skills. Training, specialization, and experience on the job result in greater productivity and therefore, economic efficiency. The net effects are higher real incomes and a higher standard of living. In other words, workers are much happier by virtue of having less leisure time.

Consumer behavior has also furthered the conservation cause. For one thing, game animals are at low risk when people hang around the house admiring the engraving on their firearms and discussing ballistics. Animals everywhere benefit when hunters fail to sight in their rifles. More birds are saved by poor shooting than by all the hunting restrictions and bag limits put together. Thousands of birds might never live to reproduce if hunters invested in a few boxes of practice shells before the season. And numerous noteworthy fish gain valuable experience in the art of escape from an inept or rusty adversary.

Then there is safety. It is dangerous to shoot in urban areas. Casting in the back yard can damage a perfectly good fly line or ruin the rhododendron. It is better to wait until you are in the presence of a guide before taking out the gear, since he is paid to accept such dangers.

In fact, guides welcome certain degrees of incompetence. No guide likes to suffer the embarrassment of sports who can turn over a size-eighteen Hendrickson in a northwester, who can roll-cast across fifty feet of current and hit a dragonfly casing in the thorax, or who shoots triples on grouse. They would prefer to observe the casting prowess of folks who fish one week each year, a source of considerable amusement. The unique casting styles employed and improbable targets associated with casted lures are anything but boring.

Guides understand that a skilled and knowledgeable public would substantially reduce the demand for guides, resulting in bands of lodge loiterers and reprobates. Many men would not survive the withdrawal.

Congress, well aware of the spending patterns of outdoor enthusiasts and of the inherent benefits, has ignored legislative efforts to shorten winter. Extended periods of inclemency allow people enough time to pore through mail-order catalogs and warm themselves in front of sporting-goods displays. Needless purchases of outdoor gear are symptoms of exposure.

Given the many virtues of conspicuous consumption, it is probably not necessary to point out similarities that do exist between standard gear and the expensive stuff, but a few remarks are in order.

I once overheard a sport ask my father to elaborate on the difference between a $30 rod and a $130 rod. "The biggest difference," he explained, "is that you are out an extra hundred bucks when the $130 rod gets caught in the screen door."

It was a thoughtless remark, not only in light of the comments made here, but because he nearly betrayed an important source of revenue for sporting camps. Unbeknown to the sporting public, commercial lodges receive annual fees from rod manufacturers based on the number of screen doors located on their premises, guest volume, and average spring tension. Dad should have known better.

Many product similarities are obscured by price differences. If you slam the camp door on your deer rifle, you can screw up the sights regardless of make and model. Salt water will corrode firearms, reels, and rod guides regardless of cost, although in general is less damaging than lending. You can miss an easy shot on a woodcock with any shotgun. Your hunting dog doesn't much give a damn what brand of ammo you are shooting. Neither does your wife, for that matter, except at the end of the month when the credit-card bill arrives.

If you could buy all the improvements made to open-face spinning reels in the past thirty years for what they are worth and sell them for what the makers claim they are worth, you could make big money. Backlashes still occur. Bail springs still break. But the single most important characteristic of a good reel, the smoothness of the drag, is virtually impossible to determine while the reel is new and without line. You have to buy the reel and spool it with monofilament to find out if it's any good or not. Smart merchandising.

The basic difference between two-wheel- and four-wheel-drive vehicles is that owners of four-wheel-drive vehicles get mired farther from the main road.

The common boat bailer, jackknife crafted from a plastic jug and used in virtually every watercraft in North America, cannot be improved upon. Its shape and composition make it both efficient and versatile. Guides bail their canoes with them, answer the periodic needs of metabolism, and scoop up lake water to quench their thirst. They do not rust or rot, and they last for years if you keep them from blowing out of the boat on the highway. Because of their inexpensive nature, consumers are asked to contribute to the economy by purchasing bleach or antifreeze.

The essential difference between standard equipment and the best money can buy is, of course, the price. And that should be reason enough for owning the finest.

Ducks

A surge of wind sliced through the blind and sent ripples up Jack's spine. His fingers wiggled inside the gloves in an effort to maintain feeling while numbness pulled at his toes. Across the bay nothing moved except the sun's rays dancing over distant stretches of water, and one desultory crow. The decoys shifted uneasily, also tired of waiting.

It had been over two hours since daybreak when they had set out the blocks, their muscles tight with enthusiasm. But the warmth of the cabin had long since deserted the flesh, and soon the memory also. Other than a pair of mallards roused in the half-light as they motored across the flats, not a duck had stirred. Even the seagulls had gone somewhere to warm up.

It was the guides' day off, and Andy and Mark had invited him to join them for some duck shooting. Both men sat huddled a few feet away, training their eyes in opposite directions, saying nothing. Andy's yellow Lab, Sam, lay trembling by his feet, sending puffs of steam across the blind. Another belch of arctic air swiped at the cheeks. *And they call this fun?*

"Guess I'll pull the boat up," said Andy. "The tide's been coming pretty good since six, and we don't need that bobbing around."

"While you're out, I might as well get rid of some coffee.

Not much danger of a duck arriving right now." Mark leaned the muzzle of his twelve-gauge against the woven sedge and poked around for a cigarette. Lighting it, he reached out and hauled the shotgun back in.

Five minutes passed, then ten. Neither guide moved a muscle. Sam panted, still shaking. *What about the boat?* Jack mused. *I guess Mark doesn't have to go all that bad. I'm building up for something, myself, but I suppose it'll hold for awhile. Geez, ain't it cold!*

"Want me to check the boat?" Jack offered, hoping for a chance to get some circulation in his body.

"Not yet," was the terse reply.

Jack looked down at his frozen pant legs, again pulled on the zipper of his coat to make sure it was all the way up. Bits of frost had appeared on his barrel.

"Nothing is going to light in here today with that wind from the northeast," said Mark.

"Damn right," said Andy. "We should have known better than to set up here in the first place. Let's pull the decoys and go down by the mouth of Rocky Brook."

"You get the boat while I yank in those two closest blocks with my waders. It wasn't my idea to come here!"

"Oh, shut up, for Christ's sake. I'll pull that furthest string of blocks, then pick you up, if you haven't drowned by then." Andy's voice was loud and angry.

"Your outside mallard is afloat anyway," snapped Mark, "the one with the short anchor line. I thought you were going to put some more cord on it. Better get it quick before it drifts off."

"Wind up the lines *right* this time, dammit. This is no day to pick apart frozen lines."

"I will if you shove the bow over so I can grab the hen. I don't have six-foot arms."

Yet, neither man moved. *Great,* thought Jack, *Here we are in the middle of nowhere with loaded twelve-gauges and these guys about to lose it.*

Suddenly a pair of mallards pitched into the decoys. Mark swung onto the first one and dropped him instantly. Andy killed the second just as the bird wised up, desperately trying to pick up some air. Four more ringnecks set their wings from the right, and the blind resounded with thunder as three of them belted the water in separate explosions. The fourth flew off a hundred yards and lit, obviously hit. Andy quickly threw another shell into his gun and swung on a single teal scaling past the rear at red-line velocity. The green-wing buckled, its momentum carrying it into the bushes somewhere over by the boat. "Nice shot," Mark grunted.

Samantha danced around the blind, waiting for the signal, but Andy's hand was palm side down. "Two blacks, low on the left," he warned. "Freeze."

The ducks flared when they saw the dog, but it was too late for the closest one. Mark's gun sent the bird end over end, hitting the bay in a tumble just beyond the sets.

"Okay, Sam, go get 'em!"

The blind came to life as all three men stepped out to survey the damage. Jack noticed he had forgotten to eject the last spent shell.

"That was some flurry! I think I hit the lead ringneck. By the way, what was that argument all about?"

Andy took a mallard from Sam's jaws, gave her a pat, and sent her back out.

"Oh, nothing," answered Mark gently. "Ducks only come in when you're picking up the decoys. There's nothing wrong with their ears and they're pretty smart, so you have to be damn convincing."

Camp Cooking

O utdoor cooking is basically the same as indoor cooking, with minor differences. These include such challenges as rain and wind and sleet; the necessity of finding dry firewood; the irritations of blinding woodsmoke, mosquitoes, and deer flies; roots and rocks that constantly trip you up; and the pitfalls of primitive furniture. There is also the danger that someone will try to help you cook.

In my neck of the woods, guides cook a full shore lunch every day. This consists of potatoes and onions, the day's meat, part of the morning's catch, and coffee. On top of this we have homemade bread, pie, and cookies from the lodge kitchen. It is a tradition in overeating that serves as a welcome break at midday.

Many lasting friendships began around a campfire. The shore lunch offers a moment of intermission from life's rigors. Guides and their sports shed any pretensions they may have, and discuss the world as equals. They interpret the fishing, tell stories, and solve the nation's problems. It is a time for lightening up, a breather for those in the fast lane.

Guides do everything in their power to make certain the shore lunch doesn't get screwed up. Burnt pork chops or a soggy butt can dampen the outdoor experience and take the magic out of the day. You want to put together a perfect meal with little fuss. This is relatively easy if you are vigilant. But it is never a given.

The first thing you need is good, dry firewood. Wood is abundant in the Maine woods if you are willing to hunt for it, and carry a sharp axe. Sports often volunteer to collect firewood for the guide, which explains why you wind up with a pile of wet wood, rotten logs, green branches, old bark or hemlock. Hemlock crackles a lot and burns about like sheetrock. In the time it would take to cook an edible meal with fuels like these, you could bring electricity to the site.

If you visit public campsites along popular canoeing rivers, such as the Allagash in northern Maine, you will notice the scarcity of burnable wood. Overnight campers rake these areas for firewood so they can sit around the bonfire at night. It is apparent that most woodgatherers are willing to walk about 150 feet from the campsite in search of wood, whereupon they turn and circle their way back. Wood is readily available to anyone willing to walk 151 feet into the forest. Guides prefer to avoid such areas, and it has nothing to do with firewood.

One of the greatest challenges for any camp cook is to guard his good firewood. People love to watch a fire. They will sit around in the evening with a jug of Old Overcoat and burn anything combustible for the sake of flame, and without much thought for tomorrow's breakfast. At shore lunches the sports like to get a big fire going long before a potato has been peeled or a fish cleaned, leaving little wood to cook with once things are ready. You can frisk them for matches when you hit shore, but it doesn't go over well.

An unwritten law of the woods is that you never touch another man's axe. It dates back to a time when one's livelihood depended upon a strong back and a keen blade, and it is honored today among guides and woodsmen. A guide won't even touch his colleague's axe.

This explains why a guide sometimes gets a little uppity when someone unknowingly picks up his axe and begins pounding driftwood on a nearby rock. Near the sporting village of Grand Lake Stream lies an ancient burial ground where generations of guides have interred the bodies of sports who made this mistake. Some of those people died of contusions to the cranium, but most of them had their throats slit.

My canoe axe has passed down through several generations of guides before me and is now a family heirloom. It was used by my great-grandfather to cruise timber along the St. Croix and by my grandfather to hew out canoe stock for Grand Lakers. My father kept it razor sharp over a long and notable guide career, handing it over to me when he turned eighty. The axe is so old it has had seven different handles, and three different heads.

Extreme weather conditions can make cookouts interesting. Light rain is not a problem, but a steady downpour gets tricky. By the same token, a little draft to coax the fire along is fine, but not when the draft has been christened by the National Weather Service.

Unlike the Sunday picnic, shore lunches aren't canceled on account of weather. People wonder if we can get a fire started some days. It's a reasonable concern, given that the entire lunch requires cooking, you are nine miles by water from the nearest landing, and it is raining like hell. That you will manage somehow is linked to the fact that you, too, want to eat.

A similar explanation applies to frying fish. Sports usually notice that guides like to fry perch, bass, trout, etc., at the shore lunch. The truth is, guides like to eat perch, bass, trout, etc. Guides are quite willing to eat the product of other competent guides. Rookie guides should bear in mind, however, that when veteran guides insist on doing the cooking, it is not always for instructional purposes.

Dealing with the weather is an everyday part of guiding, especially so during meal preparation. Top priority is to choose a lunch site where you are not likely to be abused by the weather, and second is to make your people as comfortable as possible. This means finding some lee and, perhaps, shelter. An old broken-down woods camp can seem like the Ritz on a rotten day.

On Spednic Lake we have a lunch ground called "the Sandbeach" that affords great protection from a northwest

JUST HANG IN THERE A BIT LONGER 'N YOU'LL GIT THAT FISH FRY I PROMISED!

blow and which is easy on both the canoe and clients when unloading. This is a great hideaway, unless Ralph is already there.

Ralph came from New York thirty years ago. He bought himself a boat and got his guide's license, but never lost his Brooklyn accent. He discovered the Sandbeach lunch ground in his rookie season and thereafter felt he had a warranty deed to it, never considering that another guide, who perhaps helped build the site, might like to use it once in a while. Ralph cannot hear a damn thing but makes up for it with conversation. His jokes are 1960s vintage and, let's say, politically incorrect. His cooking methods came from "Mark Trail," and he uses his fingernails to pick meat out of his teeth. He's a nice old guy, like the Ralphs of other lodges, and the other guides enjoy him. But how attractive the Sandbeach is really depends on the severity of the weather. If you are guiding the Archbishop of Boston and his wife, it might be better just to go somewhere and string a tarp.

The day's weather can help you predict a lot about lunch. Chicken, for example, requires a long, steady flow of heat to cook well. This makes it easy to guess what meat is packed if the heavens open up around lunchtime. Bev Weatherby argues that if the chicken comes out black and crunchy on the outside and raw in the middle, everyone is likely to find some of it to their liking. My father used to say, "On days like this, Son, they'll eat anything." He and Bev got along real well.

If it's 95 degrees in the shade, and you decide to lunch with another guide, it'll be your turn to fry. You can bank on it.

Potatoes and onions are the staple of shore lunches in Washington County. They are as predictable as the sunrise. You can eat them boiled, fried, baked, or in a chowder, but you can't sit down without them. Even the local ravens who clean up the lunch sites have developed an affection for potatoes and onions, so long as you don't boil the onions.

One time I was guiding with Homer Clough and my brother Lance in a party of six men. Homer is a small man but could have eaten competitively had there been official contests. For one reason or another the party did not eat onions. They were probably from Texas or someplace down South where they have a mindset on biscuits and gravy, or scrapple, or some fried dish, but for whatever reason would not touch the onions. We had a big potful boiled up and Homer had perched on a rock midway between the fireplace and the table. By mutual agreement Lance and I forked an extra two or three onions onto Homer's plate each time we tended the sports, which was often. He would decline vehemently, but eat them nonetheless.

When lunch was finally over, Homer stood up, his stomach distended four inches over the belt. By all reckoning he had consumed a dozen or more onions. His men told us that night he didn't even bother to start his motor after lunch, chugging and sputtering his way to the landing using only his paddle as a rudder.

Making do in the Maine woods is part of the charm and mystique of being there. In order to get to places where nobody else is, you need to travel light. This means restricting the dunnage to what you can carry in a knapsack or canoe. Anyone who brings a lot of paraphernalia has never had the pleasure of a half-mile portage. Waldo Brooks used to say that the length of a canoe carry depends on how much you are shouldering.

We each carry an old mail sack full of pots and pans for cooking, and refer to this as the *wangan bag.* It doesn't take much to boil a pot of coffee or whip up some cornbread. The inside of each bag is blacker than black, and a real hazard to anyone reaching into one of them. Sports often poke fun at the black, crusty pots, and your hands always look like Cajun food, but what other color might one expect? Nothing gets the soot off, short of a cold chisel.

My father was guiding a wealthy couple years ago on Big Lake. They were part of the old Philadelphia upper crust, and the woman was not used to roughing it. She constantly complained about the flies and the canoe seat and the morning's fishing, and by lunchtime Dad's patience was strained.

When the meal was ready and placed on the table, the woman glanced contemptuously at the black pans and muttered, "This food isn't fit for a pig!"

Abruptly, my father replied, "If you wait a minute, I'll find you some that is."

The quirks of Mother Nature give outdoor cooking, and outdoor dining, added dimension. Overall, they make the experience better, not worse. There is nothing like the sound of waves against a rocky shore and the call of a distant loon to spice up a meal, or the scent of balsam and pine to whet the appetite. Nor is there a better garnish than good company.

To Stop a Dog from Barking

T his is a gruesome little story that will, no doubt, be offensive to some readers. It can be argued that the account does not even belong here. Many dog trainers do not share Dan Bean's philosophy in the handling of particularly obstinate hunting dogs. Nevertheless, his technique is effective. The story is told, therefore, for instructional purposes and because, after all, it did happen.

First of all, you have to know Big Dan. He is a huge man of over 300 pounds, most of it north of his belt, and the upper-body strength of the Hulk. With a full beard that obscures most of his face and a paucity of front teeth, he casts a pretty imposing figure in the stern seat of a Grand Lake canoe. He weighed better than 430 when he and I first guided together, and provided better shade around the lunch ground in those days. You never wrestled Big Dan for your piece of pie, but you made damn sure you got to it before he did.

Big Dan is also perhaps the gentlest man I know. He has a great affection for children and animals, and keeps a small casual farm where he surrounds himself with barnyard critters just to enjoy them. When he's not guiding he harnesses up his two Belgian workhorses and gives hayrides at the local fairs. A couple years ago the local game warden brought an orphaned fawn to Dan's farm, figuring it was the deer's best hope for survival, and Dan and his lady friend nursed and cared for the deer until it could make it on its own.

Big Dan doesn't drink and rarely cusses, although he has no objection to those who do. He's been there. His mild demeanor governs each day, which he takes one deliberate step at a time. You can hear his bold tenor within half a mile of the Topsfield church most Sundays, and he'll entertain sports with the occasional hymn between fish. His major ambition is to become an old-timer, and he'll reach that milestone long before the rest of us. He also has a passion for hunting raccoons.

One October evening about twelve years ago, Dan figured he'd go for a little coon hunt.

As he pulled into Rick's driveway, it was already way past dark. In the headlights he could see Rick waiting on the front steps with his big blue tick.

"You ain't gonna bring him, are you?" Dan asked over the noise of the engine. "He'll be right in the way, as usual."

"Yup, I want to take him along so he'll get the hang of it." Rick grunted as he brought the hound around the truck.

"That one ain't never gonna get the hang of it! He's the most useless idea of a coon dog I ever saw. Leave him here, and we'll just hunt my dog."

"Dammit, Dan. It's *my* dog, and I want to take him. How else is he going to learn?"

Dan sat in the cab sulkily while Rick put his dog on the short body of the old Scout and fastened him to an eyebolt. The engine groaned. A minute later the passenger door opened and Rick got in.

"You know he'll just be a pain in the butt," Dan continued. "He's more stubborn than you are."

"He isn't either."

Big Dan pondered the remark as he backed the pickup out of Rick's driveway, found first gear, and started up the road. The night was clear and each hedgerow tossed dark shadows onto a moonlit field.

Rick was an out-of-stater recently settled in Topsfield, having married a local girl, and was eager to fit in. He had managed to rescue a couple of half-grown hounds from the county humane society and now considered himself a coon hunter. He didn't really have a clue but provided company when the regulars couldn't hunt. His blue tick was now fully grown. The dog had a massive, boney head wholly lacking in gray matter, two sets of bow legs, a questionable nose, and a voice powerful enough to rattle every storm window in Topsfield. Rick called him "Dawg."

"What do you say we just hunt Jack?" Dan offered as they drove along. It was more of a statement than a question. "When he picks up a scent we'll let him go until he trees a coon. At that point, we'll take Dawg and walk him in to the tree and let him loose for a while. If the coon is big enough, we'll enlighten him some more."

"Okay," Rick muttered.

The last time they had hunted together, Dawg had refused to stay on the trail, running back to the truck every five minutes and baying non-stop until the other dogs got messed up and lost the scent.

Dan's black and tan coonhound was unleashed and set out ahead of the Scout as they poked along the old Codyville road. Before long, Jack let out a yip and darted across the ditch, nose wagging. Dan pulled onto the shoulder and shut the engine off. The big blue tick let out a salvo from the truck body.

Pretty soon, word came back from Jack. He was working an overgrown apple orchard not far from the road, but had not yet straightened out the coon's departure trail. On each report, Dawg would answer with a long salvo of his own, and then continued to bay for no particular reason other than to hear himself. Before long, Jack's bugling was drowned out in the much closer and louder bays of the big blue tick.

"Rick, you've got to get that dog to shut up!" Dan commanded. "I can't tell where Jack is, with your dog sounding off like that."

Rick fetched up hard on the hound's collar. "Dawg, keep quiet."

He may as well have spoken to the moon. The dog struggled against Rick's grip, letting out a series of bellows. Rick shook the dog's head, swearing in earnest. The hound craned its neck skyward and howled with greater fervor than ever.

"I'm telling you, Rick, do *something* to keep that dog quiet!"

Dan paced up and down the edge of the road, training his ear to the distant yelps of his coon hound. The big blue tick continued to bay from the truck body, filling the valley with a confusion of echoes and destroying the concentration of every living thing.

In desperation, Rick brought his flashlight down on the brow of his hound. It was one of those heavy six-battery jobs, and made an audible thud as it struck home.

"Shut up, Dawg!"

The impact was enough to cause most dogs to pause and reflect. Not Dawg. He didn't even seem to notice, sending forth another round of brawling howls. Any feelings of remorse Rick may have had were short-lived. He struck the dog again, and the hound responded with even greater intensity. The noise was deafening, interrupted only by a breath of air between bays.

Exasperated, Big Dan jumped across the ditch and strode off into the woods. He called off his dog and returned to the truck with Jack on leash. A few minutes later they were headed east on Route 6 toward the town dump. Neither man spoke.

Finally, Dan broke the silence.

"You know, Rick, I think I can teach that dog of yours some manners."

"Really? I'm about worn out trying."

"It will take some discipline to quiet him down. But he needs the right approach. What will you take for him, Rick?"

"Geez, Bean, I don't really want to sell him. I must have thirty bucks in him in grub alone."

"Would you take fifteen? I'd really like to give it a try, but I'd want to own the dog if I'm going to devote myself to teaching him anything."

"To tell you the truth, he ain't much good to me the way he is. How about twenty?"

Big Dan squirmed over onto one cheek and hauled his wallet out of his back pocket. Fingering through the wallet, he pulled out a twenty and handed it to Rick. After some hesitation, Rick slowly reached out and took the twenty. The truck slowed up to turn into the dump, where many a coon hunter stopped to pick up a fresh scent. Dan stopped above the bank, his lights shining out over a mountain of garbage and debris.

"He's my dog, right, Rick?"

"Yeah, he's your dog." Rick glanced at the twenty-dollar bill. Dan extended his right hand and they shook on it.

Dan opened his door and went to the rear of the truck, unfastened the blue tick, and walked him to the front of the truck by the left beam. He pulled out his .22 Colt pistol and put a bullet through the dog's head. Picking the dead animal up in both arms, he carried him down over the bank and laid him in a hollow. Then, as a second thought, he walked over to

an old, wooden stereo console someone had discarded, picked it up and set it on top of the dog.

"Jesus, Bean, you shot my dog!" Rick wailed as Dan got back in the truck. "I can't believe you just killed my dog!"

"No," said Dan as he nudged the lever into reverse, "I just shot *my* dog." Rick looked down at the twenty still clutched in his fingers. "Now, Rick, let's go chase a coon. Mitch told me there was an old cronger hanging around his chicken coop last night. I guess those hens were real upset. Mitch said they never laid a single egg for him today."

Rites
of Passage

t is reported that a lady once asked Admiral Byrd, upon returning from one of his expeditions to Antarctica, to describe his most difficult accomplishment there.

"Madam," he said, "the hardest thing to do at the South Pole is to take a leak with seven layers of pants and nine pairs of mittens."

Byrd's experience is familiar to outdoorsmen. But I dare say the challenges women confront in the wild are even greater. I'm not qualified to expound on the latter in any great detail, although some knowledge of the female predicament has come without solicitation.

I was guiding a matronly woman and her adult daughter in August and chose a small island for lunch, mainly because it offered high ground and afforded a nice view of the lake from the campsite. Upon climbing the knoll, both ladies hurried off along a trail behind the fireplace and to the left while I began bucking up some firewood.

Now, some sports do not know this, but guides also have to rid themselves of excess fluids from time to time, and one custom is to wait until the clients have thoroughly removed themselves from the vicinity, whereupon the guide steps off to one side of the clearing and relieves himself. It makes little sense for everyone to travel if the purpose is privacy. Lodge guests have told me in confidence, and with some amazement, that their guide did not "go" once during the day. In actual fact, they did not see him go.

On this occasion I gave ample time for the gals to seek their niches of comfort and security before selecting my own route, which was to the opposite side of the clearing. Thinking discretion the better part of valor, just in case they were whizzingly fast or fast at whizzing, or whatever, I decided to step inside the curtain of foliage.

Suddenly the brush started crashing and the limbs snapping, and I stopped to see what huge animal approached. It was the mother, who had circumnavigated the entire island to find her spot not ten yards away from me, She whirled and dropped her pants so quickly I could do nothing except freeze and pray I was invisible. The loudest noise was the thumping in my chest. The view was not particularly exciting.

What saved me was that, upon completion, she pulled herself together and immediately burst off in the direction whence she came. When it was safe, I completed my mission and stepped back into the clearing, washed up, and started lunch. About ten minutes later the two of them returned by the same trail on which they had left, probably thinking they were on an island the size of Newfoundland. And no, I did not say anything.

Another time, on Baskahegan, we lunched near an old woods camp. The man was off to the woods the second his feet hit terra firma, while his wife inquired about an appropriate destination for her. I instructed her that behind the camp was fine, since it was seldom used, and then only during deer season. She was not especially comfortable in the woods, and I don't think she realized that the only portions of her body concealed by the corner of that camp were her face and kneecaps. The image comes back to me now and then.

The convenience of bodily function was not handed out evenly between the sexes. Men are much more privileged anatomically in discharging fluids than are women, a theme that is clearly evident during blackfly season. To duckwalk through a cedar swamp with a thousand flies in hot pursuit is enough to make any woman bitter.

The intimacy of a twenty-foot open guide canoe doesn't make it easy for women, either. Sandwiched between a husband who is captivated by his fly rod and a guide whom she knows only casually can cause a woman to be overly polite. Too often she broaches the subject of shore leave only after experiencing considerable discomfort. She keeps searching for the right choice of words, and the more she has to go, the harder it is to find them.

Last summer, Bob Kay was guiding a young couple from Tennessee. About three o'clock the lady indicated to Bob she "needed to go to the bank." Twenty minutes later she asked him "if he minded if she went to the bank." Thinking their finances none of his damn business, he told her that was fine, and went about his fishing. After another fifteen minutes went by the woman blurted out that she "needed to go to the bank *right then.*" It finally dawned on Bob that she intended to make a deposit, whereupon he headed for the nearest shore with dispatch.

It should never be this way. A woman's darkest fear must be laid to rest at the very outset as a matter of courtesy. After all, guides do not have iron bladders and appreciate a pit stop themselves once in a while. Young guides are known to sit for hours with their eyes jaundiced and their knees locked together, too embarrassed to say anything. They eventually smarten up, if they don't explode first.

Men, of course, are fully capable of passing water in the boat and do so without hesitation when in the right company. It is a curious notion how a man who would take a leak in the presence of his wife, and who would take a leak in the presence of a guide, will generally not take a leak in the presence of both. Yet, on other occasions he will relieve himself with almost comic eagerness, consumed in mellow reverie.

I hate to see a guy haul it out and aim over the rail, without any thought for the safety of the boat or its passengers.

The male ego causes many men to misjudge their capabilities. They fall short on trajectory, lack good valve control, and underestimate the height of the gunwale. They stand up to compensate for anatomical deficiencies and leave a trail across the bottom of the canoe. They lose their footing and forget all about the end of the garden hose as they try to regain it.

These efforts are interesting enough in the high rollers, but to see the guide crouched low in the stern while white-knuckling the rails to keep stability is discomforting. Too many drowned men have been pulled from the icy depths with their flies open.

Canoeists sometimes wet their paddle, extend it past the gunwale, and take a leak on the blade. It works well. A guide, accustomed to his own personal paddle, often fails to mention the technique. He would prefer to pass the boat bailer to the fellow in need.

If you use the bailer, make sure the cap is on tight. Bob Coxe, a dentist from Pennsylvania, didn't. He requested the bailer one morning but failed to notice we had removed the cap. He unzipped his trousers, laid his hat on the seat, and proceeded to gaze across the lake, at cloud formations and seagulls and islands. Meanwhile, a freshet streamed out the nozzle of the bailer and directly into his hat. After his friend and I recovered from our mirth, Bob applied a liberal dose of sunscreen to his bald spot, and we trolled his hat the rest of the morning.

Incidentally, the boat sponge doesn't work as well as the bailer.

On a cold, rainy day a guy can use the bailer inside his poncho to avoid the risk of exposure to the private parts. Big Dan runs a finger down the inside of the rim to tell when it's full. I prefer just to check it now and again.

It is remarkable how chilly days accelerate the metabolic process. The principle that matter cannot be created or destroyed does not hold true on raw days out in a boat. The human body will generate three gallons of liquid from a single cup of coffee. I guess it has to do with physics.

Obviously there are times when trips to the shore are

unavoidable. These occur with regularity, and their urgency is a pretty fair omen of how well the fish are biting. About the time you hit the mother lode, time out. The bigger the fish, the greater the emergency. I know. I've screwed up more good bass spots than I care to remember. If the salmon are going bonkers, you are probably miles from land and can barely make it. Sometimes you don't. Or else the only shoreline around is windblown and boulder-strewn, forcing you to travel extra distance to go ashore. In any event, the fish have usually quit by the time you return.

The best that can be said for those uncontrollable impulses, whether they occur while you're out in a boat or in your chest waders, is that they usually correspond to the feeding frenzy.

Retrieving Dead Deer

The buck was getting heavier with each step, and the rest stops were now coming two or three minutes apart. They had dragged it maybe seventy yards since the last stop. As if the weight and bulk of the deer weren't enough, his antlers were catching on every stump and log and hummock along the way, making it miserable work.

"Time out," said Waldo. "I think your deer needs a rest. Let's take five." He straightened up and let out a big sigh. "I reckon he'll go two hundred pounds, all right. Are you going to mount this rack when you get home?"

Jeff didn't answer immediately. His breath was coming hard, and a trickle of sweat rolled down the side of his cheek. "No," he panted, "I don't plan to. Who needs another set of antlers hanging on the living room wall?" He was mighty proud of this buck and couldn't wait for the boys back home to see the monstrous rack. He didn't want to let on to the guide, but this was his first real trophy.

"I'm going to find a nice stick," Waldo said. "It'll help us get this deer out."

The guide propped his rifle against the deer and sauntered off through the black growth. Jeff had read about ways to tie a deer's head and front legs crosswise to a stick, making the animal much easier to drag. Pretty soon Waldo was back with a four-inch hunk of dead maple, about two feet long.

"Ever shoot a twelve-point before?"

"Sure," Jack lied, "got some pretty heads like this on the wall at home."

Waldo raised the club above his head and with a couple of mighty swings lopped both antlers off the deer's head.

"Good. It's a lot easier dragging a doe. Grab that leg and let's get going."

Jeff started to say something, but the words wouldn't come.

A guide is normally expected to help the sport get his deer out, an exercise in brute strength and ignorance that is simplified considerably if you are heading in the right direction.

The intellectual challenge usually comes in finding the beast after it's down, since carcasses have a way of moving about. If you are lucky, you heard the shots and can pretty much figure it out.

The problem occurs when a greenhorn comes and gets you to fetch his deer. More often than not he failed to get any decent landmarks in his excitement, ran like hell all the way out, and now doesn't have a clue where the deer is. He only thinks he does. This becomes great fun if the deer was shot in a ten-year-old clear-cut that is coming back in softwoods, in which case you have to actually step on the animal to find him. It might be easier just to go shoot another one. But you never kill two deer unless you are lost, since this will bring a game warden in about ten minutes.

If you are real lucky, the guy didn't drag it after it was dressed. It is better not to add a hundred yards to the distance home. It is also nice not to go looking for the heart and liver, which most flatlanders—having been brought up on pork chops—leave with the entrails. They think it looks yucky, but it is likely to be the only part of the deer *you* taste.

Deer always run downhill to die, so that you can drag them uphill afterwards. It has something to do with getting the last laugh. For variation, they sometimes pick the middle of a bog. The deer shot under the old apple tree in the back field where you can drive right to with the pickup occurs but once in a lifetime.

There is little difference between the best way to get a deer out and the worst way, if you have to do it by hand. In the north Maine woods the terrain is uneven, the deer heavy and the going tough. The old method of tying the deer to a pole and carrying him on your shoulder works great if you are guiding two linemen from the Green Bay Packers in full game pads and they agree to do the lugging, and they can stand the deer swinging wildly on each step, and you don't mind ducking a few shots on the way out. Otherwise, you'll wind up dragging the deer, either with a hooked stick in his jaw or a rope around the neck, and it will get old very quickly. You may wish to try other methods if the deer is illegal, in which case you probably don't intend to hang him outside the house.

A few years ago my sister-in-law hit a cow moose with her car several miles north of Danforth on Route 1. The state trooper, who happened to be female, wrote up the damage report but was disinclined to finish off the moose, which lay injured about fifty feet off the road; it was getting dark and she was accustomed to shooting human silhouettes. My brother finished off the animal with the help of her .38.

The moose was awarded to my brother, who then called several of us to help him drag it to the road. Hauling a dead moose is a lot like dragging your car when the brake pads are frozen to the drums. We would not have tackled it had it been fifty-one feet, and the next time we'll measure.

During the whole fracas one of the locals, Frank, kept saying how much fun it was. By the time we got the moose out it was pitch black. We were soaked in sweat and moose hair, bruised from stumbling around in the dark, and kind of sorry we had missed supper. Pete finally asked Frank what was so much fun about it.

"Well," he said, "this is the first moose I've ever been mixed up in where you didn't have to whisper."

Before hauling any beast out of the woods it is prudent

to think over the best route. It may not be the Bataan, but it will seem like it. Furthermore, you don't want to be told of a shorter route once you get back to town.

Speaking of shortest routes, I once paddled some fellows an hour up a small trout stream when suddenly a pulp truck roared by, not thirty feet from the brook. I wasn't aware that that country was being logged, and when asked about it I simply said, "Well, er, uh, you, mmm, see, ah. . . ."

It may be useful to discuss orientation with your party. Point out how the sun usually sets in the west, if you can still see it, and how much harder it is to find your way home after dark. Everyone should agree that their compasses still point north, and never mind the declination stuff. Some sports are not too confident of magnetic north after they leave the shoulder of the main road. You want everyone pulling in the same direction.

A fundamental law of motion is that the best walking is in the wrong direction. The most direct route always involves blowdowns, brush piles, steep slopes, water, thorns, or all of the above. This is true whether you are trout fishing, bird hunting, deer dragging, or lost. Then again, you are not as likely to shoot a nice deer in front of the A & P.

Numerous items are recommended for making it easier. These include everything from surveyor's ribbon for finding the deer, to ropes and hatchets and bicycle drags and parachute cord. Neat new things that a hunter can't live without show up in the gun shops every fall. One problem is that you need a trailer to get all this stuff into the woods with you; another is that the more you prepare for a deer, the less likely it is you will shoot one.

Why is it those guys who always write the stories about big bucks in magazines never mention the fun of getting them home? They forget some of us don't own off-road vehicles.

They never describe the delight of getting a branch poked in the eye, of straining until your groin pops or your knees buckle. They never show pictures of your sleeves dripping in blood or the shirt stuck to your sweaty back, or of a guy dragging a deer with one hand while his other carries the rifle plus all the coats he has shed. They never have any infra-red shots of you trying to hang the deer up after dark, or any photos of your supper solidifying on the top of the stove. They never write about tough-eating stags or the fact that your wife and daughters hate venison.

A lot can be said for not getting your deer.

A Lack
of Communication

S ometimes guides and their sports have trouble understanding each other. They use different idioms. Terms
and expressions get all twisted around, and words take
on entirely different meanings. Out-of-state dialects and ac-
cents create many problems for us local boys, who have
enough difficulty understanding each other.

Several years ago the State of Maine tried to interest
Berlitz in sponsoring an extension course for natives, to help
them understand how out-of-staters speak. The firm worried
that it might be asked to explain how out-of-staters *think,* and
didn't want to get into that. Accordingly, guides have been left
to work out communication problems on their own.

Whenever phrases do not translate easily, guides resort
to facial expression or body language. This partially explains
why guides spit so much. There are many gestures that have
universal meaning and these can be useful, particularly if
someone loses a big fish.

I have found that if you work with your clients on
proper speech, they will eventually get the drift. It just takes
time.

Take "Give it to him!" for example. Guides use the expression when they want their client to set the hook on a fish that has been running with the bait. Sports commonly respond by giving more line to the fish rather than striking. Had the guide wanted the fish to run longer he would have said, "Give it to him." Sports falsely take this to mean "yank," not noticing the absence of the exclamation mark. No wonder sports screw up so many fish.

One time a man was backing his boat into the water at a remote landing and asked me to watch his rear. I could see that the skeg on his new outboard was about ready to fetch up on a big rock. When he asked me if it was okay to keep backing up, I told him "Go ahead." I can't help it if he didn't listen to me.

It's especially difficult to explain where you want people to cast. Sometimes you have to provide a nine-digit ZIP Code. After a dozen or so casts have failed to come anywhere near the stump you are pointing at, you suddenly realize the people just don't understand.

Deer hunters have trouble grasping when and where it is everyone is supposed to meet up. I suppose they have their watches set to Greenwich Mean Time, which explains why they are never at the rendezvous point when you are. Some guides find it helpful to erect billboards on designated logging roads that simply say "Here."

Novices are not familiar with many standard sporting expressions. Guides avoid such terms as "break your firearm" or "break down your rod" when they loan equipment to clients. Fishing guides are always "throwing a fish back," but in the hour before lunch this refers to the floor of the canoe behind the stern seat.

Requests from clients get misconstrued. When people say they would like to get off the lake to make a telephone call during normal business hours, guides presume they mean before dusk. "One last cast," on the other hand, means they want to fish through the night. "Could I try one of these deer-hair bugs I tied?" suggests they can handle a fly rod a damn sight better than you. "I'd like to go ashore" should be understood to mean "Now!"

One June morning I was fishing for bass on the lower end of Spednic Lake with two older gentlemen. I can't remember their names or where they came from or even what they looked like.

The only thing I remember is that the fellow in the bow liked to stand up to cast. It wasn't the right day for ballet, and I wanted him down. We had a south wind, not bad but building up for something. I was fishing a lee shore, and although the wind was not too evident to the men, it was a nuisance to me. I was constantly fighting the canoe to keep it from sliding in and out with eddying wisps of air coming over the trees, so the men could comfortably face the spawning structure.

I have learned that people who stand in a canoe usually have a hearing impairment. It was true that day. I mentioned that he was no longer thirty, but he apparently didn't hear me or else didn't believe it. I suggested that he sit down on the casting thwart, installed for that purpose. I also explained that his profile acted like a sail, making it very difficult to control the canoe. He sat down.

Now, I enjoy swimming, but I generally prefer to pick a warm day when I have time to put on some trunks and take off my boots. The plan that day was to fish, and I knew we could lose a lot of productive fishing time if I had to stop to right the canoe and dry out all my worldly possessions. It can be downright inconvenient.

The next moment, he was back up. His body quaked in a constant struggle to maintain his balance, and each time his muscles tensed we could feel the quivers all the way back to the stern. He muttered something about how much easier it was to cast and how long he had been fishing. His chum and I made eye contact.

I again asked him to sit down. It's an instruction my springer spaniel has no trouble understanding. He sat down. Thank you very much.

Two minutes later he was up again. I gave him a couple minutes, then told him it was impossible to see rocks coming up on the bow—the ones I wanted to fish—with him standing. It was hard enough to pick things out in the glare, even with

my Polaroids, but no way could I see through him. Sullenly, he sat down again.

This time he was good for all of ten minutes, but on the next strike he popped back to his feet. The bass threw the plug when he rose, but the old guy stood there flailing as if the fish was stupid enough to bite again. I allowed it was time to re-phrase my request.

"Look, if you don't plunk your ass in that seat right

now, and keep it there, I'm going to put you out on this island. Maybe you can share supper with the son of a bitch I left there last month!"

Either his hearing improved or else he was more familiar with my choice of words.

Casting Aspersions

I don't know why sports like to pick on their guides. I wonder if they say nasty things about other people when they're home.

Charlie Smith is a longtime guest of the lodge and sort of an institution here. During his many years fishing Washington County, out of different camps and with many guides, he has come to know a great deal about life around lodges. Charlie is nobody's fool. His body is hobbled by polio suffered as a youngster, the problems having been compounded by several bad falls, and he uses two canes to get around with. But his mind is sharp, honed by a career on Wall Street, and his tongue is quick to size up a situation.

One spring I was breaking in a new chore boy at camp, and was having limited success at it. On one particular day he managed to screw up the oil mixture for all the rental motors, forgot to fill kindling boxes in the camps, and then painted all the door and window trim on a camp with the wrong color. It wouldn't have been half so bad if he had gotten as much paint on the wood as he got on the new screens. On top of all this, he backed one of my boat trailers into a pine tree and broke the rear light.

The guests were assembled in the lobby that evening, relaxing and relating their experiences from the day's fishing.

Charlie thought it was a good time to counsel me on the new chore boy.

"You know," he began, "young Joey is too goddamn stupid to be a chore boy. Why don't you see if you can make a guide out of him?"

I could see the eyebrows rise on the new guests. Charlie has a way of making it hard for one to either agree or disagree with him.

George Bush, Jr., also one of the regulars, often comes to fish about the same time as Charlie. As the result of a bad car accident, George received brain damage that impaired his motor skills and he uses a wheelchair part of the time. He can get around slowly with the use of a cane and a foot brace, but it requires considerable effort. His brain, however, is fully engaged and he is far more intelligent than most of us. George's

"MY GUIDE, MITCH, THINKS ROE vs WADE ARE TWO WAYS TO FISH SALMON IN A STREAM."

sense of humor has enabled him to surmount many obstacles.

George often accuses me of using "guidespeak" in my fishing instructions, and once encouraged me to pick up a Maine/English dictionary for translation purposes. This usually occurs about the time he loses a nice fish, at which point he begins referring to me as "what's his name." I don't know how long I have to take this.

Once in a while, if things are busy and there is a shortage of guides, I'll take both Charlie and George with me salmon fishing. I must be masochistic. Andy refers to us as the nine-legged canoe, factoring in all the canes.

A few years ago the three of us were trolling on the northern reaches of East Grand, when we were stopped by the New Brunswick rangers. They are the province's equivalent of game wardens. It was a routine check, so we had our lines reeled in and were digging out our Canadian fishing licenses for their inspection.

George, who has a slight slur in his speech as a result of the accident, started talking to the head ranger.

"Forgive us if we've done anything wrong, sir," he pleaded, " but this is the handicapped canoe . . . two physical, one mental."

It's awfully hard to defend yourself when your day's pay is riding on good client relations. Whenever people pick on your adroitness, or instincts, or cooking, or garb, it's best just to accept it. After all, they didn't hire you to disagree with them.

Ed Zern was perceptive enough to understand that career opportunities are limited in the back country. In *To Hell with Hunting* (Appleton-Century, 1946), Zern said, "The truth is, most guides are not smart enough to hold down a steady job at the local sawmill, and are obliged to choose between guiding and burglary. And although burglars meet a better class of people, the hours are not attractive."

Unfortunately, guides have been victim to many false accusations, and the records have been allowed to stand. My friend Walter Morse recently told me a story that should help clear things up.

It seems a local guide was working in the Boston area last winter, planning to come back north around ice-out. At a dance one Saturday night he met a young lady and they hit it off rather well, spending most of the evening together. He asked her if she would like to go out with him the following weekend, and she consented eagerly.

"Where are you from?" she asked out of curiosity.

"I'm from Maine," he said. "I'm a guide in the lake country Down East. One of my sports offered me a job down here during the off-season, so I took him up on it."

The girl's face suddenly filled with horror. She shrunk away as the words bore sharper meaning.

"I'm sorry, but I'm going to call off our date for next weekend. Please excuse me."

"What's the matter?" he asked with dismay. "Did I say something wrong?"

"Never mind," she said as she turned to get her coat. "Just forget you ever met me."

Catching her gently by the arm, he said, "Susan, you've got to tell me what is the matter. Do you have something against Maine guides?"

She stopped and looked him straight in the eye. "Yes, Arthur, I do. My girlfriends have told me all about your kind. I just can't believe a nice person like you is one of *them!*"

"Hold on, Susan. Apparently guides have some kind of reputation in these parts. What exactly have you heard about us?"

"Well, I'm not sure how I should say this," she began, reluctantly, "but I suppose you should have a chance to defend yourself. My friends have told me that guides, for want of companionship, have sexual relations with animals. I am told that you fellows are known to have sex with horses." She paused. "And cows. And pigs. And chickens. . . ."

"Chickens?" he exclaimed in disbelief.

Regulating the Bait Supply

G uides are paid to find fish and to help their clients catch them. Sure, a nice salmon on a fly rod fights better than one on eight colors of lead-core, and the explosion of a smallmouth hitting a surface plug has a magic you can't duplicate by catching it on a gadget trolled eighteen miles behind the boat. The fact remains that some people like chocolate and some like vanilla, and I don't have a problem with that. A guide should understand that there are certain things he is paid not to have an opinion about.

Catching fish on live bait is a lot of fun and beats not catching fish, whether it is your job or not. I would guide for sunfish or chub if that was a person's pleasure, and have a damn good time doing it. It may seem mercenary, in the sense that few guides would do it on their day off, but there is great reward is seeing your people have a good time. After all, that's what this deal is all about.

Guides find the traditional pecking order among anglers somewhat amusing. Why bait fishermen act apologetically among their comrades in the fishing fraternity, particularly their fly-fishing friends, is beyond me. A bass is far better off lip-hooked by a conscientious bait fisherman who sets the hook early and who releases him carefully, than by a fly fisherman who allows him to swallow a nymph and then tears half his throat out in the catching. Greed and ethics are quite divorced from matters of style and skill, but those with elitist attitudes will never come to accept it. Fly fishers like to cast, while bait fishers mainly like to catch fish. Big deal.

"Natural baits" is the term used by outdoor writers who want bait fishermen to buy their magazines but who wish not to offend their purist readers. They don't need to pussyfoot. By and large, most people who profess to use only artificials will defer to bait under the right circumstances—i.e., when it is the only way to entice a fish to bite and when they are safe from the scrutiny of their cronies. Guides refer to these fishermen as the "artificial people."

Guides have carried bait since the days of Izaak Walton and are knowledgeable in its presentation. There is certainly much to learn about bait fishing. Guides instruct their clients in technique and even bait their hooks. The "artificial people" refer to guides as master baiters. Enough on semantics.

During the bait season for smallmouths, guides pick up the nightcrawlers, minnows, frogs, crayfish, and whatever early in the morning before they meet their party. These are normally purchased from a bait dealer or obtained from the sporting camp where their clients are staying, in which case the bait is billed directly to the sports.

Guessing the right amount of bait to take is one of the profession's greatest quandaries.

Suppose the guide does not take enough bait and the bass bite like crazy and he winds up running out. Sports start talking strangely when this happens. They begin reciting the number of miles it is from their home to here, and tell you all about the purpose of their trip and stuff like that. They give you personal stats on the cost of their vacation and how difficult it is to get time off. Then they mumble remarks concerning your intellectual prowess and Oedipus complex, all in the same breath. They start casting wildly, and further than normal, and much more often, and retrieve at twice the normal speed. You begin to sense they are annoyed. This is not a good time to talk about your family or, for that matter, anything else.

The opposite risk is taking a pile of bait only to find that the bass have lockjaw. Whether you bring the extra bait home or they die in the bucket is academic. The sport winds up with a hefty bait bill that does not correspond to the two shiners he fished with all day, and this—on top of the lousy fishing he had—really sets him off. You learn a lot of the words they use in more civilized places, get accused of being part of some great conspiracy, and discern something about the fellow's opinion on prices and incomes.

Guides are gun-shy. At sporting camps, guides like to return what bait they didn't use, revise their client's bait invoice accordingly, and then dust it for home. This would seem fair. Except that a bunch of minnows that have been swished back and forth in a bucket all day, fondled by asphalt fingers, hooked in the back, and starved for oxygen usually last only another six minutes after getting dumped back in the bait box. Camp owners love this, as it makes their bait enterprise a real profit center.

The usual guide strategy, therefore, is this: You take what you think is a reasonable amount of bait, then regulate the rate of depletion during the day to coincide with the amount of time left. Optimally you should have enough to see you through, but never anything left over. This way everyone winds up happy, except the bait.

Bait regulation is really simple. The guide, as grand marshal and chief steward of the bait buckets, has full control since he allocates the bait to his sports. It's just a matter of brushing up on input-output analysis, queuing theory, and personnel management. Which policies are selected depend on whether the bait situation is in surplus or deficit. Then you just try to implement the measures as subtly as you can.

Let's first consider the situation where *the bait supply is too low* and hopelessly inadequate for the rest of the day. With good planning this will not occur until after nine o'clock in the morning. Conservation measures are called for immediately. These include rationing, recycling, fishing disruption, etc.

Rationing works well if the bait is such that it can be subdivided into smaller units, such as nightcrawlers. Instead of putting a full nightcrawler on their hooks you give them halves, then quarters, then worm segments. The sports always notice the chunks getting smaller, but you explain it is for reasons of economy or that the bass want a small bait, which usually gets you out of it. Bisecting the frogs may cause dissent from both the sports and the frogs.

Note that this type of rationing is far different from that intended to bias the success of the anglers. For example, a guide may save the best bait for the good wife of the occasional selfish son of a bitch who has caught seventeen smallmouths to his wife's one and who would like the ratio to be twenty-five to one. You might even salvage his marriage, but only for a while.

Recycling means that all the bait goes back to the bucket regardless of its condition, usually under the guise of R & R. The contempt you risk from running out of good bait is not as severe as when you run out of bait altogether. So long as there is something to mush onto a hook, there is hope.

In surveying the minnow bucket, guides mentally sort the shiners into four classes: alive, sort of alive, dead, and decomposing. When the stock is low, you throw away nothing. The sort-of-alive minnows show definite signs of weakness, such as swimming tight circles on their sides, and are terminal patients. The dead ones are beyond the medical capabilities of a good vet, but once in a while give a muscle spasm and retain some trace of their original colors. When hooking on a bait that is decomposing, you should suggest to the sport that he "work" the rod.

It's a test of compassion when you have only six frogs left in the bucket and each one has two or three hook holes in his jaw. Every time you open the bucket they all look up as if to say, "Take Billy, it's not my turn." Nightcrawlers never evoke the same sense of sympathy. Given the fine aroma you get from dead worms, saving them takes real dedication.

An equally effective method to bring the dwindling bait supply into equilibrium is to slow down the fishing. This must

be accomplished with guile. Beating the gas can on the bottom of the boat or wildly flailing the water with your paddle can result in a career change. Pounding the anchor on a rocky bottom works but is amateurish, since you might as well drift out of the school while the anchor is lifted. Veteran guides have an anchor line long enough to allow them to surreptitiously drift off the spot without detection.

If the bait supply is in emergency status you should move, giving the pretense that you would like to find some bigger fish. Then you choose a series of sterile spots, all of which look about the same to the sports. Finding fishless habitat is not particularly challenging, although some guides are better at it than others. If you ever see a guide fishing such places and you know his bait supply is okay, it tells you something about his sport.

I recall overhearing a conversation my father had with two young fellows as he was pushing away from the landing one morning. It was their first fishing trip to Maine, and they were obviously excited.

"Ten bucks says we catch over twenty-five bass today," offered the Old Man.

After a few moments' consideration, during which time they sized up his experience, they decided it unwise to take my father's wager.

"In that case," he said, "ten bucks says we don't catch a single thing."

Another way to slow down the rate of catching, thereby reducing bait consumption, is to put on the least effective baits. There are always a couple of giants that the bait man used to make his count, and these can be used to discourage the average bass. At the same time, you keep the biggest chub from eating his buddies.

The same theory applies if you debilitate the bait so it is less attractive. If you squeeze a minnow until his air bladder pops or give a frog a little whack on the head, each of which can be done with your hand inside the bucket, it will tend to slow the action. Those who are less sadistic can simply drag the bait through a little pool of reel oil or DEET set aside for that purpose.

George Bush, Jr. and I were fishing the St. Croix River, anchored over a bunch of pretty decent bass, when I glimpsed a canoe coming down the stream. I reeled up, and as soon as we were able to get rid of George's fish, we removed all the bait from our hooks and let the lines back down. We tried to look as bored as possible as the canoe got closer, now followed by half a dozen others. It turned out to be a boys' camp, spending a week's outing on the river. Just as we were telling the trip leader how terrible the fishing was, a three-pound bass grabbed George's bare hook, whereupon he yanked and the bass came flying to the surface. We didn't land the fish, but when I noticed that not a single boy carried a rod, it made me feel pretty small.

Obviously, if you do run out of bait the whole game changes. It then becomes appropriate to bad-mouth bait fishing and elicit the virtues of catching fish on artificials, particularly working the angle of personal achievement for deceiving the fish. Either that, or take your party on a mission to dig up some more bait, but that's another adventure.

The problem of *having too much bait* sets in motion a similar array of countermeasures. The inventory must be drawn down in a conspicuous fashion so that the sport fully appreciates how much is used. In that way there will be no quibbling later on.

The prodigal mode calls for the guide to discard any bait deemed passé by consensus. Use the same squeeze and whack methods described earlier, bait up their hooks, then point out how sluggish the bait seems. Offer fresh bait as often as practicable, use generous portions, and double up when the bait is small.

You can also increase mortality. Don Wallace conveniently forgets to change his water, although he recently learned that a little gasoline works just as well. John Gaskins likes to impale the bait a little closer to the spine. John Trainor would parboil the bait in the hot sun, then open the lid with expressions of shock and surprise. Arthur Christie would simply pinch the heads off the frogs with his hand over the gunwale. This way they didn't float around the canoe and rouse suspicion, and Arthur made it home in time for supper.

Sports will assist the drawdown with a little encouragement. By suggesting long casts and hearty wrist snaps you can liberate enough bait to boost a lake's forage base. Get them to release the line late in the cast, so that the bait enters the water at the speed of sound. Have distance competitions. Hook the bait lightly for best results.

As a last resort, go find a bunch of bass. The trouble with this approach is that it is now late in the day and the bait supply is nearly exhausted. You probably only have a couple good frogs or crayfish left, not counting the escapees that are under the gas can. If you locate some nice fish the sport gets excited, forgets to open his bail, and the frog heads over the horizon at warp speed.

Mission accomplished. Time to head in.

About the Author

DALE WHEATON grew up in eastern Maine, where his parents operated sporting camps. Like his father, grandfathers, and brothers before him, he learned to guide at a young age. He was educated at the University of Maine and the University of Nottingham in England, and taught economics in the "off-season" at the University of Maine. He and his wife, Jana, operate Wheaton's Lodge in the remote village of Forest City, Maine. They have two daughters.

About the Artist

DAVID WHALEN is an illustrator and graphic designer who lives in Lucerne, Maine.